The **WOW** Factor Workplace

"Anyone tasked with helping an organization create an irresistible experience for its employees will find this an insightful read. Pages are chock-full of stories, experiences, and tips from well-known executives in corporate America who helped create and nurture workplaces that have the 'WOW factor.' Soak it all in!"

—LINDA RUTHERFORD
SVP & Chief Communications Officer, Southwest Airlines

"As I learned in combat, success depends on unleashing available talent and resources. Current leadership models are failing miserably to meet this goal. *The WOW Factor Workplace* is a powerful springboard to replace outdated thinking and find a better way that lasts."

— COLONEL DEBRA M. LEWIS (US ARMY, RETIRED)
and Founder of Mentally Tough Women

"*The WOW Factor Workplace* is filled with lessons learned from strong leaders, lessons of what to do and what not to do (sometimes even more important!). I encourage young leaders looking to catapult their careers to digest every word, soak in more than just what the words say … look beyond the ink. Adjust your sails and benchmark from history and your future colleagues!"

—DONALD W. STAMETS
General Manager, Flagship Solage – An Auberge Resorts Collection

"*The WOW Factor Workplace* is full of engaging stories about best in class organizations with amazing cultures. I was inspired by the valuable leadership lessons in this impactful book."

— RUTH BRAJEVICH
Vice President, Strategic Intiatives, Ware Malcomb

"In this book you'll find invaluable insights to how people in different industries, coming from different backgrounds, have used the following principles to create successful WOW factor workplaces: Respect each person as an individual and as a member of the team; encourage positive communication with and among members; listen to understand what is being said; speak with clarity when giving guidance and direction; and follow-up … it's the real breakfast of champions."   —LIEUTENANT GENERAL BENNETT L. LEWIS (US ARMY, RETIRED)

"I LOVED THIS BOOK! In my prior senior leadership roles, I welcomed a 360 review on two occasions and thought we had a WOW entity. In hindsight, and with the assistance of the examples in this book, I can see that we were delivering on expectations and providing the service we promised, but were not achieving the WOW across the board for employees or customers. As this book articulates so well, the challenge I once found so exciting shifted to frustration. Our team leaders were providing inconsistent messages, a tolerance for mediocrity existed in the field, and some felt I and other executives had unrealistic expectations. The environment eventually grew toxic until one day I moved on, much to their relief as well as mine."   —CARYN SIEBERT, JD
former President and CEO
(Risk and insurance claims executive and independent board member)

"While you may be able to realize your full leadership potential on your own, why take the chance? Deb Boelkes has distilled the wisdom of her long and varied career into a punchy book full of wit, insight and easy-to-apply lessons for a highly successful business life."

—NEAL FREEMAN
Author, *Skirmishes*

the WOW

Factor
Workplace

How to
Create a
**Best Place
to Work**
Culture

Deb Boelkes
with Foreword and Soundbites by
Mark Goulston, M.D.

BUSINESS WORLD RISING, LLC

The WOW Factor Workplace
How to Create a Best Place to Work Culture
© 2020 by Deb Boelkes. All rights reserved.

Book Consultant: Judith Briles, The Book Shepherd
Editor: Barb Wilson, EditPartner.com
Cover and Interior Design: Rebecca Finkel, F+P Graphic Design

Library of Congress Control Number: 2019914564
ISBN trade paper: 978-1-7340761-0-3
ISBN eBook: 978-1-7340761-1-0
ISBN audio book: 978-1-7340761-2-7

Business | Leadership | Management

First Edition
Printed in the USA

To Taylor, Skylar and Mackenzie:
May you always love what you do.

Contents

Foreword

Every time Apple introduces a new Apple product, or Tesla introduces a new Tesla model, or Marvel introduces a new superhero movie, most people go WOW!

And what does WOW mean? It means:

- That's amazing!
- That's astonishing!
- That's unbelievable!

What if every time the top talent you wanted to attract came into your company and said *WOW*? What if every time one of your employees was asked by a friend, "What's it like to work at your company?" your employee replied, "I think I won the lottery!" Of course, this friend might also ask, "Are you hiring?"

Think it's not possible? Think it doesn't exist? Think I'm living on another planet or stuck in a time warp back to workplaces that existed long ago, but not in the WIIFM (What's-In-It-For-Me), loyalty-is-for-fools world?

Think again.

That is why being a part of *The WOW Factor Workplace* book WOWED me. And I know it will WOW you.

Still unconvinced?

If so, I'm guessing you might agree with the following:

A skeptic is reluctant to believe. A cynic is someone who refuses to believe.

A skeptic is someone who once believed and was disappointed. A cynic is someone who once believed and was deceived and maybe even devastated. But deep inside all skeptics—and even most cynics—is a deep ache to believe again and not be disappointed, deceived, or devastated.

If you have that ache, you will come to believe as you read the wonderful stories in this book. You will see how it's possible to create a workplace that not only WOWS everyone who works there, it WOWS everyone who hears about it.

You will discover how you can create a workplace where the best and most talented people line up to get in.

WOW is within your reach. In fact, it begins as soon as you turn this page.

—Mark Goulston, M.D.
Talking to Crazy: How to Deal with the Irrational and Impossible People in Your Life

ONE

The Best-Ever Boss

Make each day your masterpiece.
—JOHN WOODEN
American basketball player and head coach
at the University of California at Los Angeles

Have you ever said to yourself, "If only I could jump out of bed excited and eager, with a can't-wait-to-go-to-work attitude… it would be like winning the lottery?"

I remember a time or two during my career when, instead of jumping out of bed with a can't-wait-to-get-started spring in my step, it was all I could do to drag myself out of bed to face yet another day in an organization where hardly anyone seemed enthused or happy, including me.

Isn't it interesting how the last twenty-plus years of your life seem to have come and gone in an instant, but spending a day in an organization that drains the life out of you can seem like an eternity?

Have you ever had to fake enthusiasm when talking about your workplace with others or when you were looking in the mirror, getting ready for the day?

Know what I mean? It's called feeling trapped.

Isn't it strange how, in the beginning, you found that organization so alluring and promising? Once upon a time, it seemed as though it was the best workplace ever. You admired their mission, their reputation, their people, their products, and their services. You eagerly anticipated having new and interesting experiences there. The culture seemed so exhilarating that the compensation was just icing on the cake. You truly believed working there could take your career to new heights. You couldn't wait to get started.

What happened?

Well, as with any great romance, your love affair with that workplace eventually came down to your relationship with the people there … especially with the boss.

At some point, you no longer felt supported or appreciated. The challenge you once found so exciting shifted to frustration. More and more you noticed inconsistent messages, a lack of communication from above, a tolerance for mediocracy, a lack of transparency, unrealistic expectations. The environment eventually grew toxic. You came to dread Mondays. You lived for Fridays. You and those around you stumbled and grumbled along until one day the boss moved on—or you moved on, much to your relief.

It's amazing what can happen when you have a great boss.

A true saying: People join companies and leave bosses.

Then suddenly, with a new boss in place, your dread turned to enthusiasm and excitement. Instead of days dragging on and on, months zoomed by. Now you were working in the zone—the WOW zone. Every day when you went to work, you pinched yourself because you felt you had won the lottery.

Why? Because that sense of WOW didn't fade. It only got better.

Now you had a great place to work…a best place to work…a WOW factor workplace.

It's amazing what can happen when you have a great boss. Even more amazing is the kind of WOW results that can occur when your great boss has his or her own great boss. The WOW factor can spread like wildfire.

Here, when someone asked you about your job, you could honestly and enthusiastically share, "I am so lucky to have such an amazing manager. I work with the best team. I love my job. I'd never want to work anywhere else!"

Leaders in a WOW factor workplace are invariably praised as being best-ever bosses who inspire those around them to be the best they can be.

In this book, you will hear from some truly exceptional "Best Place to Work" award-winning bosses who have been consistently praised by their teams and recommended to Dr. Mark Goulston and me as the epitome of best-ever bosses. You will hear the personal leadership philosophies of these best-ever bosses, and you will learn what they did to create their "Best Place to Work" cultures. You'll learn the secrets of what makes a "Best Place to Work" company truly a best place to work.

We call these organizations WOW factor workplaces.

Most importantly, you will discover how you, too, can become a best-ever boss.

But first I'm going to let you in on a little secret: Dr. Mark Goulston inspires and energizes the heck out of me, much like a best-ever boss would do.

Granted, I don't report to Dr. Mark, nor do we even work in the same organization. We partnered up a few years back specifically to collaborate on this book. I feel truly blessed to have such an amazing colleague.

My respect and admiration for Dr. Mark stem from his extraordinary ability to read people. He has this sixth sense that allows him to somehow get right to the heart of almost any challenge someone is dealing with.

To be honest, his innate power to see below the surface and understand whatever I'm struggling with—and then use the perfect words to describe what I'm feeling even better than I can—is a bit disconcerting at times. He keeps me on my toes.

Still, Dr. Mark never makes me feel undeserving or less than I am. To the contrary, he not only accepts me for who I am, he also recognizes the many gifts I possess, and he encourages me to make the best use of them. That's why I want to work with him. He WOWs me and gives me hope that maybe someday his unique gifts will rub off on me.

I'll tell you a story about the first time we met.

I had already read Dr. Mark's first two best-selling books, *Get Out of Your Own Way* (co-authored with Philip Goldberg and published in 1996) and *Get Out of Your Own Way at Work … and Help Others Do the Same* (published in 2005). Both books, in my humble opinion, were spot-on self-help business tools. When his now international best-selling book *Just Listen* was published, I jumped at the chance to read it. It was so stunningly insightful I knew I had to meet him.

Shortly after that, I learned Dr. Mark was to be the keynote speaker at a women's leadership conference in Santa Monica, not too far from where I lived. This conference seemed like the perfect opportunity to meet him.

Anticipating heavy rush hour traffic on the morning of the event, I hit the road early to ensure I wouldn't be late. It turned out that I was one of the first attendees to arrive. As I made my way down the lobby stairs to the conference registration desk, I noticed a very polished and professionally dressed dark-haired man coming up the stairs toward me. I immediately recognized this gentleman from his picture on the *Just Listen* dust jacket. Indeed, it was Mark Goulston, M.D. I smiled, eagerly extended my right hand, and introduced myself.

I don't recall the exact words I used, but I essentially told him I was dying to meet him because I thought his book, *Just Listen*, was the best leadership book I had ever read, even if it wasn't categorized as a leadership book. I explained how I had come to this conference in order to meet the man who had such incredible insights into dealing with so many kinds of people in various types of challenging situations. I told him how I honestly thought every business leader in America should read his book.

I will never forget what Dr. Mark said in response. He simply smiled sheepishly and said, "Wow. You make me want to be a better man."

That statement struck a chord in me at the time, and it has stuck with me ever since.

Think about it. Isn't that just what great leaders, great teachers, great coaches, great teammates, and certainly best-ever bosses do? They make you want to be a better person. They inspire you to be the best you can be.

Let that sink in for a moment.

Great leaders, great teachers, great coaches, great teammates, and undoubtedly best-ever bosses are enthusiastic, inspiring, and supportive mentors. They motivate and energize just about everyone around them, from their peers to those above and below themselves on the organizational chart, to be the best they can be. They see a spark in others, articulate a vision, and kindle a desire in those around them to develop

> We don't have to be superstars or win championships. All we must do is learn to rise to every occasion, give our best effort, and make those around us better as we do it.
>
> -John Wooden

their talents and give their best efforts to achieve the vision. These inspired folks, in turn, influence others to become better in the process, too. The magnificence grows and becomes contagious. It creates a WOW factor.

A WOW factor workplace doesn't necessarily have to be in a business setting. To the contrary, WOW factor workplaces can be found anywhere: oil fields, football fields, battlefields, schools, universities, civic organizations, social clubs, church groups, and beyond.

I'll give you an example.

During my freshman year in college, I attended the University of California at Los Angeles (UCLA). This was at the time when basketball coaching legend John Wooden was head basketball coach there, at the zenith of his career. I was lucky enough to win a seat in the UCLA basketball season student ticket lottery.

While I didn't personally know Coach Wooden, it was a real thrill for me to attend each home game coached by the legendary leader lovingly referred to as the "Wizard of Westwood." My freshman year happened to be the season Wooden coached the UCLA Bruins to win their NCAA Division One national championship for a record-setting seventh straight season.

How exciting it was to watch this best-ever coach and his WOW factor team play in perfectly synchronized harmony on the floor of Pauley Pavilion. No other team in history has ever come close to winning so many championships in a row.

One of the great players on the Bruins team at the time was the 6'11" Bill Walton, a now retired basketball player and sportscaster. Walton had this to say about his legendary coach shortly after Wooden's passing at age 99 in 2010:

> He was happy with his choices, happy with his sacrifices, and he was happy when other people were happy. He never pushed

anything on you. He was not your friend. His job was for you to get somewhere you couldn't get by yourself...

He always said, "Make each day your masterpiece." He had the ability to deal with a problem, adversity, suffering; he was able to make people be their best. When I left UCLA and joined the NBA, I became the highest-paid athlete in the history of sports, and my quality of life went down. That's how special it was to play for John Wooden. The sad part is that, while we were doing it, we had no idea.

Over the years, the legendary John Wooden was recognized numerous times for his outstanding achievements. He was enshrined in the Basketball Hall of Fame in 1960 for his success as a player, and then again in 1973 as a coach, becoming the first person ever to be honored as both a player and a coach. In 2003, John Wooden received the Presidential Medal of Freedom, the nation's highest civilian honor.

The amazingly humble John Wooden had this to say about staying true to one's self:

When a person changes, he or she usually ends up with a feeling of superiority. I didn't want that to happen to my players, and I didn't want it to happen to me. I was flattered when one of the coaches at the NCAA convention introduced me by saying, "John is no different after winning ten championships than before he won one." That made me feel good because I want to practice what I teach.

Leaders must be enthusiastic and really enjoy what they are doing.

One of my personal favorite Coach Wooden leadership quotes is this:

I'm convinced that regardless of the task, leaders must be enthusiastic and really enjoy what they are doing if they expect those under their supervision to work near their respective levels of competency. With few exceptions, an unenthusiastic leader will keep those under his or her charge from achieving their collective best.

Throughout his life, Coach Wooden served as an incredible role model, not only to his team but to me and so many others who were lucky enough to observe him coaching the Bruins team. Even if I only had the chance to watch him from my courtside seat all those many years ago, and only eventually came to know him later through all I read about him and by him, his heartfelt example has long inspired me to be a better person.

While few of us will ever be so lucky to have a Coach Wooden in our lives or have a manager who makes us want to be a better person, those leaders and colleagues who do inspire us to make the best use of our God-given talents typically have their own unique ways of going about it.

Inspiration comes in many forms.

One of my personal best-ever bosses, Betty, came early in my career, although I didn't realize it at the time. Looking back, what made Betty such a WOW factor for me was the fact she encouraged me to take on a role I didn't think I was suited for, and she would not take *no* for an answer. She saw a spark in me and coached me. She created a safe environment where I could refine my skills.

At the time, I was a senior systems engineer at AT&T Information Systems (a company no longer in existence). Having already proven myself as an individual contributor, I was assigned to be the technical expert dedicated to supporting the top sales rep in the district, Phil.

In my eyes, Phil was a terrific sales guy. He could sell anything to anybody, although not everything he proposed to our customers was necessarily doable with our standard set of product offerings. It was my job to make sure whatever Phil sold was adequately designed and installed on schedule to perform as, or better than, expected. Fortunately, I had a good working relationship with the research & development gurus at Bell Laboratories. Somehow, working together with the real geniuses at Bell Labs, we always found a way to bring Phil's ideas and customer commitments to life.

One day, out of the blue, Phil quit. Poof...gone. Left without a sales rep to manage our accounts, I took it upon myself to reach out to our customers, to let them know I was still there for them and would make myself available to handle whatever they needed until a new sales rep could be assigned.

To my surprise, Phil's sales manager, Betty, offered me Phil's job. I never saw that coming.

Stunned, I thanked her for the opportunity but explained I wasn't cut out to be in sales. I didn't believe I could do what Phil did. Phil was fearless when it came to cold calling. He could communicate easily with people he had never met before. Effortlessly, he could make friends for life. I didn't believe I could ever do that.

Now it was Betty's turn to be stunned. "Debra, you obviously don't know why Phil was so successful," she stated. "It's all because of you."

I responded incredulously, "Because of me? Are you kidding? I go in after Phil opens all the doors. Then I get to work to figure out what the customer needs, which, as you know, isn't necessarily what Phil had proposed. I do what any good technical support person is supposed to do. I make sure we deliver solutions that solve our customers' business problems, on time and within budget."

"Precisely," Betty exclaimed. "The reason our customers buy from us is because of you. You can still be you, only better, as a sales rep. Perhaps you don't realize it, but Phil made way more money on commission than you ever will on an engineer's salary. If you were to become the sales rep, you could be compensated more appropriately for what you already do so well. You'll be great at sales." She saw something in me that I clearly did not see in myself.

To make a long story short, Betty coached me through it all and even offered me a 100% salary guarantee for a short period of time. Sensing my unease, she gave me a safety net by promising I could always go back to being a senior systems engineer if things didn't work out.

So, I finally agreed to give it a try, and the rest is now history. Betty was right. Not only did I earn way more money on commission, but like Phil, I became the top sales producer in the district.

With her vision and persistent encouragement, Betty changed the trajectory of my career. I even became a better leader and coach to others as a result. Never again was I afraid to take on new challenges, thanks to Betty. I didn't know it at the time, but looking back on it now, it's easy for me to see Betty was one of my best-ever bosses. I keep in touch with her to this very day.

Fast forward about fifteen years. By this point, I was leading a professional services and consulting organization for another global technology company, Arrow Electronics. One day out of the blue, another unit within the corporation, a software-as-a-service business,

Focused Fitness

5733 Saint Joseph Ave. Stevensville, MI 49127

10 Fitness Clases

was shut down literally overnight due to unprofitable operations. Every employee in that organization was terminated without notice.

This now-defunct unit's customers were understandably upset due to the fact their component engineers had come to depend on this software service to perform their jobs. Without any advance notice, without any continuing service commitment from Arrow, and confounded by the lack of any other viable alternative being readily available on the market, irate CEOs from across the country immediately contacted our chairman, demanding Arrow get back in the game.

From our Board of Directors' perspective, this software-as-a-service business was a financial drag on the corporation and not sustainable. Moreover, since they had already laid off the entire business unit, the company had no option to hit the "undo" button. The only response our chairman could give to these customers was an apology.

As you might imagine, our chairman's response didn't go over well, especially not with the multinational accounts doing millions of dollars in business with Arrow each year. A substantial number of our largest customers quickly determined their only redress was to award a significant portion of their other ongoing business with us to our biggest competitor. This retribution had a rapid negative impact on our core business—and that got our Board of Directors' attention.

I got a call from my VP boss, Cathy, informing me the Arrow Executive Committee had selected my consulting organization to assess whether there was any possible way for Arrow to profitably deliver some kind of software solution to satisfy these customers. My team was granted thirty days to figure it out.

I had learned by now to never say *no* to such opportunities. My team would have to think *way* outside the box. It helped to know we had the confidence and support of the Executive Committee. If nothing else, they would certainly be keeping their eye on us. This was a high-visibility opportunity.

I hear you are fearless!

Over the next thirty days, we met with the senior executives of each of the largest impacted accounts. When we met with them, the first thing we did was apologize for what had happened. We explained Arrow's objectives and listened to their full list of concerns, functional requirements, and expectations. Together, we prioritized their *must-haves, nice-to-haves*, and *can-live-withouts*.

In the end, my team came up with a very novel approach. The Executive Committee agreed to move forward to develop and test our proposed conceptual design with a few hand-selected customers who were most anxious for a solution. To everyone's relief, the proposed solution was a hit, and we found a price point that worked for all concerned.

Arrow won back virtually all the business they had lost and then some.

Looking back now, I must give a great deal of credit to my VP boss Cathy for having such confidence in our team from the outset. She stood up for us to the Executive Committee and convinced them to take the gamble. She put her own career on the line.

A short time later, our entire executive leadership team and all the sales organizations from across the company assembled at a large hotel in Dallas for our annual sales conference. As we excitedly waited in the lobby for the ballroom doors to open for the kickoff of our multiday sales planning session, I noticed someone rushing through the waiting crowd, headed in my direction. It was the company president, Fran. I certainly recognized him, even though I had not yet had a chance to meet him.

As he approached me, I saw a huge grin on his face. He exuberantly shook my hand and stated with enthusiasm, "I just had to meet you. I hear you are fearless!"

Fearless? I had honestly never thought of myself as fearless before.

But those impactful words instantly touched the core of my very being and informed me in no uncertain terms I now had a new reputation to live up to. I certainly wouldn't want to let our president down.

With those five words—*I hear you are fearless*—Fran sent me on a lifelong journey to prove to myself I could be fearless in the face of any challenge. Since that time, I've been on a relentless mission to inspire others to be fearless, too.

Standing there with Fran, that was the moment I realized *that's* what best-ever bosses do. They inspire their team members to be more than they ever thought they could be. They give them their full support. They provide them with recognition and applaud them when they succeed, and they enjoy the process of doing so.

As a result, team members love to work with these best-ever bosses. Their team members give their best efforts, and they make others around them better as they do it.

This is how a WOW factor workplace is made.

In this book, you won't be reading some theoretical, idealistic fairy tale. You'll learn about actual organizations that clearly possess a WOW factor workplace sense of enthusiasm. You'll learn about the real heartfelt leaders who helped make it happen.

No, you won't be hearing from egotistical leaders who take all the credit for making the WOW factor manifest. You'll hear from leaders who are somewhat embarrassed to receive any credit.

As Dr. Mark describes it: "We are talking about heartfelt *en*spirational leaders. In contrast, *motivation* pumps people up but then fades when the incentive stops. *Inspiration* lifts people up but doesn't tell them what to do next. *En*spiration lifts people up and then directs and guides them toward a vision everyone wants to make happen. Think of it as Peter Pan *en*spiring Wendy and her brothers with 'second star to the right and straight on 'til morning.'"

Now join Dr. Mark and me as we interview our band of heartfelt leaders. We'll show you a WOW factor workplace is possible and achievable by you.

When we're done, you'll be able to take yourself, your team, and your organization to a place you may have never believed was possible.

Soundbite FROM DR. MARK

Most of us live comfortably within a box of limitations. We know we are good at some things and not at others. We choose work and tasks that fit within our constraints, never dreaming we are capable of much more.

When you set low expectations, you're stuck in *yes, but...* consciousness. You agree you would like to live larger, but...

A real stretch goal is something that springs from within —an internal desire to be or do something you aren't yet being or doing. When you can tap into that inner vision, it's amazing to see what you are capable of.

ACTION STEPS

1 Think about the organizations you chose to leave during your career. Why did you leave? Did your boss play a major factor in your decision to leave? What did your boss do or not do which fostered your decision to go?

2 Now think about the best boss(es) you ever had. Have you ever had a manager you would consider to be a truly great boss? What did this manager do that made you love your job? Did he or she kindle a desire within you to be a better person ... to make each day your masterpiece?

TWO

Take Their Breath Away

*An unparalleled experience for both employees and customers,
and in turn, makes both employees and customers feel special,
appreciated, and respected.*

In a nutshell, a WOW factor workplace has an inviting and
energizing culture, *esprit de corps,* and tremendous employee
and customer loyalty. When combined, they deliver a consistently
positive impact on the bottom line.

It sounds easy enough to accomplish, but it's apparently a magic
few people possess. Creating a WOW factor workplace is not a
subject typically taught in business schools. Perhaps if they did,
we would find them everywhere.

The fact is, you are likely to find a WOW factor workplace just
about anywhere, in any industry, in any region. Yet, like rare exotic
cars, you don't see them very often. This is indeed a shame because
they are a delight to behold and enjoy.

It's a little like falling in love. You might even experience falling in
love at business school, but they certainly don't teach you how to

do it in any business school I'm aware of. Still, you know it when you experience it. And it certainly doesn't happen every day.

The WOW factor workplace is a rare breed. The good news is, while few people seem to understand the magic required to create one, even *you* can do it. As the old saying goes, when you build it, they will come. Your staff will magically transform, and your customers will turn into raving fans.

Of course, as with any WOW kind of magic, being a good magician still takes practice, even once you know the tricks that create the effect. In this book, you will discover a plethora of skills that, when implemented in unison, magically create a WOW factor workplace.

Now let's look at another workplace environment that exemplifies the kind of WOW factor magic I'm talking about.

Intent on teeing up a great experience when my husband and I decided to explore Tampa, Florida, I googled *best boutique hotel in Tampa* and discovered an interesting "contemporary hotel with a culinary focus," The Epicurean. As two foodies, a stay at The Epicurean sounded like an intriguing place to try out.

Next, some friends recommended we have dinner one night at Bern's Steak House, directly across the street from The Epicurean. To ensure we would have the best dining experience possible, I researched *top ten restaurants* on TripAdvisor. Up popped Harry Waugh Dessert Room at Bern's Steak House as the number one listing of more than 1,800 restaurants in Tampa.

So, I made a dinner reservation at Bern's for our first night in town.

Upon arrival at The Epicurean Hotel, I was instantly impressed by the first-class treatment, which began as soon as we entered the driveway. The valet immediately introduced us to the check-in attendant standing right next to him, a smiling and welcoming twenty-something woman who cheerily escorted us to the lobby.

Once inside, it seemed we had entered the lobby of a chic Napa Valley winery. Two fully stocked wine refrigerators doubled as check-in desks and the wall behind was made of wooden wine crates touting the logos of many of our favorite vintners.

After handing us our room keycards, Ms. Twenty-Something escorted us to our third floor room by way of a grand tour through all the first floor points of interest. The tour included an extraordinary wine shop, a beautiful and upscale theater-style classroom where a cooking class was underway, a hip and lively

Everywhere one looked, there was evident and impressive foodie attention to every possible detail.

lobby wine bar, and the contemporarily rustic Élevage Restaurant, aptly named for its artisan comfort foods "elevated" with premium ingredients.

Passing the Epicurean Theater (the cooking classroom), I took note of the big sliding barn-style door that closed off the classroom from the lobby. The door pulls were fashioned like enormous chef's cutlery utensils. Across from the theater was a cozy sitting area and library filled with all sorts of cookbooks, all bookended by two big screen TVs continuously displaying cooking programs. This place truly promised to be a foodie's dream stay.

As Ms. Twenty-Something finally led us down the third-floor guest hallway, I noticed unique frosted glass light fixtures to the right of each guest room door. Each fixture artfully depicted a different food or wine concept (e.g., wine bottle, grape leaves, salt and pepper shaker, a wine glass).

Our guest room itself reflected a contemporary "barn & bar" culinary theme. Even the minimalistic print on the decorator pillow—artistically placed on the cool white duvet-covered king size bed—depicted a knife, fork, and spoon. A handsome bar-height counter made of chopping block wood and glass ran the full length of one wall and was nicely outfitted with a stylish pair of leather bar stools. Everywhere one looked, there was evident and impressive foodie attention to every possible detail.

Later, back downstairs in the chic lobby wine bar for happy hour, we found all the comfy leather sofas and chairs in the intimate library sitting area filled with guests sipping and munching away in convivial conversation. We felt lucky to find two open wireframe stools in the wine bar, so we took up residence there. A handsome and friendly plaid-shirted bartender quickly handed us the happy hour menu offering an impressive list of handcrafted appetizers, cocktails, and wines by the glass, all quite reasonably priced.

The small plated appetizers looked divine as plaid-shirted servers whisked them from the kitchen. Knowing we needed to pace ourselves to fully enjoy our dinner *and* dessert at Bern's, we ordered the featured red wine by the glass and exchanged some light conversation with the bartender.

Our delightful time in the lobby wine bar flew by all too quickly, but we eagerly made our way across the street for an on-time arrival at Bern's, where we were greeted by a steady stream of luxury cars pulling in and out of Bern's valet entrance.

Once inside the foyer, deep red walls and carpet, decadently flanked by ornately gilded velvet armchairs, immediately captured our attention. Before I could make my way to the only empty seat in the opulent antechamber, a dignified maître d' informed us our table was ready and regally escorted us to our assigned dining room.

On the way, we passed an opulent assortment of differently decorated dining rooms. We eventually made our way to *our* dining room, the Bordeaux Room.

Once seated, I was mesmerized by all the elegantly clad wait staff quietly yet diligently working the small dining room's dozen or so tables. As the maître d' placed the weighty leather-bound dinner menu in my hand, I was stunned by the size of it… so many pages!

> **We consider every night a big event for the restaurants, and we strive to go above and beyond our guests' needs and wishes.**
> —David Laxer, President and Owner of Bern's Steak House

The maître d' then gestured, with a suave wave of his hand, to the leather-bound book of wines resting against the wall at the end of the table. It was even larger than the dinner menu! I then recalled our friends telling us Bern's wine list was noted as one of the largest and most complete in the world.

As I reached for the telephone-book-sized wine list, I noticed the beautiful floor-to-ceiling mural that graced the length of the room. It appeared to be a historical map of the Bordeaux wine region of France, hence, the name of the room. It was almost too much to take in all at once.

The wine book was formatted with two columns of wines listed per page, categorized by region and further itemized by color, variety, label, and price. The enormity of it was mind-numbing. Before spending too much time reading the tome, I asked our waiter, "Do you have any wines by the glass?"

"Yes, of course," responded our waiter. "We offer over 200 wines by the glass. Would you like to peruse the list, or would you like to speak to the sommelier?"

"Two hundred? Wow!" I gasped in amazement.

"I'm sure I can find something suitable in here," I said as I laid my hand on the wine book. "Give us just a moment to take a look. This is really something."

I read to my husband just a sampling of the overwhelming variety of wines and regions represented. As we toured the cavernous wine cellar later, we learned Bern's stocked over 600,000 bottles and 6,800 labels. It could have taken us all night—maybe all week—to peruse the entire list.

We simply selected one of our favorite pinot noirs and called it done.

"Excellent choice," confirmed our waiter.

Next, on to peruse the dinner menu. Like the wine list, it, too, could have taken all night to read. The menu was chock-full of interesting information about beef, the aging process, and what to expect from different cuts of varying thicknesses and weights. There must have been at least sixty steaks to choose from, along with all the other types of meat, fish, poultry, first courses, and side dishes.

Amazingly, if you selected one of the many steaks, the *pre-fixe* steak prices included several preselected seasonal first courses and side dishes. The *pre-fixe* steak meals were quite a good value.

As our waiter delivered our wine, he asked if we planned to enjoy dessert in the Harry Waugh Dessert Room. "Absolutely," my husband exclaimed.

"Very good," responded our waiter. "I will make a reservation for you. Have you been to the Harry Waugh Dessert Room before?"

"No," I replied, "And we have been given explicit instructions not to miss it."

Our waiter responded, "You are in for an exceptional treat. Please don't hurry through your dinner, however. Just relax and savor your time here."

I was intrigued by the idea of going to a room dedicated just to desserts.

But I need to get back to reading the dinner menu. Taking it all in was like getting a PhD in the intricacies of ordering a perfect piece of fine beef. Clearly, Bern's goal was for guests to obtain a cut served precisely to their liking.

Bern's offered every conceivable permutation of steak preparation from very rare to well done, with or without crust, rare with a cold or warm center, and more. Its steaks were available in four thicknesses, from one to three inches, with thirty-two variations in color, juiciness and cooking time. To aid in the selection of the very best steak to suit individual palates, the menu even included a spreadsheet that Bern himself devised to describe all the options.

My husband and I were at the opposite ends of the rare-to-well-done spectrum, yet we were each delighted with the steaks we were served. My rare and crusty filet just might have been the best I'd ever had.

Fortunately, with all that steak studying, we didn't have to think about what to order as sides. Bern's had the entire perfect meal down to a science, starting with a standard first course of French Onion Soup (also perhaps one of the best I've ever had).

While wholly impressed with the food, we were just as impressed with the service from our obviously young but extremely professional and friendly waiter. He never hovered, but magically appeared the instant you wanted him, ready to attend to your every need. After finishing our soup and salads, I asked him, "How long have you been a waiter here?"

He seemed a bit embarrassed and paused before he answered, "I've been a waiter here just two weeks. Is there something wrong?"

"Oh, no. Not at all!" I quickly replied. "In fact, we've been very impressed with your professionalism. It's rare to find someone your age with such outstanding manners, attention to detail, and superior service attitude. I can't believe you've only worked here for two weeks. What did you do before you worked here?"

Our young waiter took a quick sigh of relief, smiled broadly and then confided, "Actually, I've never worked anywhere else, but I have been here at Bern's for two years now. I spent my first eighteen months working in the kitchen. That's where most everyone starts when they come here. If you do well enough in the kitchen, you might get promoted to assist in the dining room."

With that, our young black-suited waiter straightened his maroon-colored necktie and nodded ever so slightly toward an older gentleman wearing black slacks, a white short-sleeved shirt, and black bow tie, pouring water at the next table.

Bern Laxer was a firm believer in hiring for attitude, work ethic, and a yearning to learn the business. They don't hire for experience.

"He is a dining room trainee. He busses the tables in this dining room, under the direction of a dining room manager. The managers are the ones wearing suits with silver ties," our young waiter explained.

"After working the kitchen, I was promoted to dining room trainee for another six months. I wore a uniform like his until I passed the test to be promoted to waiter for this dining room. When we become waiters, we get to wear black suits and maroon-colored ties, and we are assigned to work two tables of two people, on our own.

"It would mean a great deal to me if you would tell my senior captain what you think of my service. He's the gentleman over there wearing the gold tie."

"Of course," I replied. "We would be happy to speak to your senior captain." Our waiter thanked us and quickly disappeared.

A moment later, our waiter escorted the gold-tied senior captain to our table and introduced us. He was so gracious to us that one might have thought he had nothing else to do but chat and answer our questions about Bern's philosophy for wait staff.

From him, we learned the founder, Bern Laxer, was a firm believer in hiring for attitude, work ethic, and a yearning to learn the business. The restaurant does not hire for experience. Instead, Bern's prefers to train inexperienced employees, so they don't have to break bad habits. Training starts in the back of the house, which helps everyone understand the basics of what every other employee does. This approach creates better teamwork. It can take up to two years of hard work and menial chores performed all over the restaurant before one could be promoted to wait staff.

Training starts in the back of the house.

It was very apparent to us the people who work for Bern's *love* working there. Because of this, it has some of the longest tenured staff in the industry. Our senior captain had worked there for thirty-three years. The most senior captain, Jamal, who led the Rhône Room team, had worked there for nearly forty-five years. Considering that most people don't work anywhere for forty-five years, we were blown away by the Bern's philosophy, their dedication to quality, and the staff's long-term loyalty.

The senior captain went on to explain, "After the new staff prove themselves, both males and females graduate to wearing silver ties. Only then are they allowed to wait on four tables of four guests. The most veteran servers can eventually become captains and wear gold ties, like mine. Captains oversee entire dining rooms and wait on six tables of six or more."

With that, the senior captain winked at us. "Perhaps, from what you are telling me, the gentleman here will be ready for a silver tie in a year or so, maybe less." Our waiter smiled proudly.

The senior captain then asked us, "Would you like to tour our kitchen and see the operation for yourself?"

Honored, we immediately responded with a resounding "Yes!"

"Wonderful," replied the senior captain. "Just let your waiter know when you are done with your meal, and I'll escort you to the kitchen for a tour. We'll also take you through the wine cellar. It is really something to see. After the tour, you can head up to the Dessert Room." We couldn't wait.

As promised, after dinner, our dining room captain escorted us along with a few other diners into the bright, shiny kitchen. Here, we learned the square footage of the kitchen was larger than all the dining room areas added together. Over fifty people, including sous chefs, meat cutters and salad station personnel, were assigned to work in the kitchen. Additionally, bow-tied trainees filled in at various stations while numerous black-suited waiters and dining room captains carried on a well-choreographed dance folding napkins, slicing cheeses, pouring sauces, and carrying large, beautifully displayed serving trays to and from the many dining rooms. It was a bustling, highly efficient, and well-orchestrated show.

Founder Bern Laxer firmly believed customers should have a clear view of where their food originates. Hence, they have invited diners into their kitchen and wine cellar for years. During our wine cellar tour, we learned Bern's keeps their 600,000+ bottle wine cellar at approximately fifty degrees (a bit cooler than the typical US wine cellar) to slow down the aging process for their many older bottles.

We later learned Bern's also employed even more staff to work on their eight-acre organic farm in North Tampa as well as in a large intake wine warehouse and vast storage/workshop on Howard Avenue. The restaurant uses its own staff to perform all sorts of functions, from tending to the electrical, AC, and plumbing needs, to the fabrication of the sheet metal. Their laundry department cleans and presses all the linens in-house while fabricators refinish the antiques and reupholster the chairs. Bern's was a poster child for vertical integration.

In total, Bern's employed an astounding 300+ people. Its longest-tenured employee, then at 45+ years, was a veteran mechanic/carpenter/jack-of-all-building-trades who, even before being hired by Bern, worked for the contractor who built the restaurant's first significant expansion.

Following our kitchen and wine cellar tour, we finally made our way up the opulent gilded stairway to the legendary Harry Waugh Dessert Room, which was managed as a separate operation. The Harry Waugh Dessert Room itself had seating for over 200 guests.

As large as it was, it seemed incredibly romantic and intimate, thanks to the forty-eight small, darkened, elliptical dining booths fashioned from old redwood wine cask staves, each seating parties of two to twelve. Each dessert booth had a separate sound system, allowing each party to select their favorite mood music, from jazz to classical. As we entered our cocoon-shaped booth for two, I felt as though I had stepped into an enchanting ride at Disney's Magic Kingdom.

Not to be outdone by the extraordinarily comprehensive dinner menu and Book of Wines in the downstairs Steak House, the Harry Waugh Dessert Room menu must have had dessert wines and spirits numbering in the thousands. On top of that, there must have been at least forty decadent delights on the dessert specialties menu.

My husband and I decided to go for the gold. We shared the monster dessert called the "Taste of Bern's," which provided sample-sized portions of five of their signature desserts: Macadamia Decadence Cake, King Midas, Banana Cheese Pie, Chocolate Cheese Pie, and Vanilla Cheesecake. What a way to end a glorious (and gluttonous) WOW factor evening.

The next morning, back at The Epicurean Hotel, we decided to have a light breakfast in the hotel's Élevage Restaurant. The smallest, lightest item on the breakfast menu was the Continental Breakfast, which included not one, but TWO of the lightest, flakiest, and most mouthwateringly buttery croissants I have had this side of Paris.

As I often tend to do, I captured our waiter in conversation about working at The Epicurean Hotel. He told us he loved working there and felt most fortunate to be part of The Epicurean team. His story was not unlike the one we had heard at Bern's: all Élevage Restaurant staff began by working in the kitchen, and as a result, they worked as a well-oiled team. He went on to confirm that all the staff loved working there.

> An environment where exemplary role model leaders train and inspire employees to create extraordinary products and deliver impeccable service at a great value (regardless of the price).

When I asked him if perhaps there was something in Tampa's South Howard Avenue water supply that caused the similarity between The Epicurean and

Bern's staff training philosophies, The Epicurean waiter confessed, "Actually, The Epicurean Hotel was created and founded by Bern's. There was a search for the right partners (Marriott International's premier brand) to bring their vision to reality."

Asking how that came about, we learned Bern's Steak House was booked solid during the winter seasons for years, but the business tended to slow down a bit in the months in between Florida's snowbird seasons. The Laxer family conceived the idea of building a unique hotel on its property across the street to exemplify the same standards and quality of great food, wine, and service, but with a nouveau twist. The Epicurean Hotel quickly became a foodie destination unto itself. It ultimately became so popular both Bern's and the hotel are now booked solid all year long.

I was so impressed when I arrived home from our trip, I wrote an article about this WOW factor experience for our local hometown magazine, and now I am telling you about it.

If you'd like to get that kind of WOW factor word exposure for your business, keep reading, and you'll learn the secrets for doing so.

Bern's is the epitome of a WOW factor workplace. Perhaps another way to define it is: an environment where exemplary role model leaders train and inspire employees to create extraordinary products and deliver impeccable service at a great value (regardless of the price), which creates an unparalleled experience for both employees and customers, and in turn, makes both employees and customers feel special, appreciated, and respected.

Regardless of whether it's a for-profit or charitable organization, private or publicly held, a military unit, an educational institution, or a governmental entity, a WOW factor workplace is an environment where the desires of employees and customers alike are fulfilled, time after time. The WOW factor workplace consistently receives well-deserved praise underscored by the highest ratings in social media reviews. This, of course, generates increased demand and entices ambitious people to work there.

With so many high-potential applicants, the WOW factor workplace can be extremely selective in terms of hiring, ensuring it brings on board only those candidates with just the right attitude. As a result, staff members enthusiastically sing the praises of their leaders and peers. They encourage their best friends to apply. They make their clients feel special at every touchpoint. Highly satisfied customers eagerly anticipate their next interaction, and they enthusiastically refer their friends.

If nothing happens to break the cycle, employee delight and customer loyalty continue to build indefinitely for the WOW factor workplace. The WOW factor of Bern's enterprise is especially impressive, considering the restaurant-accommodations industry sector, in general, has long suffered a notorious reputation for high employee turnover, far beyond that of many other industries.

Obviously, Bern's is—and has been for a long time —doing something extremely rare indeed.

Soundbite FROM DR. MARK

Great puts a smile on your face and maybe even puts a spring in your step but is often temporary.

Wow takes your breath away and cements itself into your memory where you pause with reverence every time you remember and reexperience it.

ACTION STEPS

1   Think about the organizations you are familiar with where employees love to work and where best-in-industry financial results are the norm, year after year. Can you think of any?

2   Think about an especially outstanding experience you had with any business or other organization. Consider the key characteristics which made that time a WOW experience for you. How did the environment make you feel?

3   What do you think made this group or organization stand out?

4   Assess the various stakeholders who might have benefitted as a result of the mindset of this organization.

THREE

Love What You Do

*A handwritten note card I would get from an
employee that said: "Thank you. You've changed my life.
This is the best place I've ever worked," is much more powerful,
much more valuable than any amount of money
I could have in the bank.*
—PAUL SPIEGELMAN
Cofounder, Small Giants Community

Face it. If you don't love what you do for a living, the workplace around you will not likely ever be a WOW factor workplace. If you are not thrilled with your contributions, chances are you will be a drag on those around you. You may not realize it, but you will pull down your peers, and you will cause disappointment to those you serve. Depending on where you are in the organization, the span of those you affect can be quite broad.

Life is too short not to spend your days doing something you love, something which inspires you, something you might even be willing to do for free if you had some way to pay the bills. If you don't love your workplace, if you are not energized and fulfilled by your role, you owe it to yourself and those around you to make a change. You really should have a heart-to-heart conversation with yourself and figure out what can be done to get more wind beneath your wings.

More often than not, WOW factor workplaces are what they are thanks to, at least in part, one or more heartfelt leaders somewhere within the organization who serve as catalysts to encourage and enable themselves and their team members to be the best they can be, doing something they love to do. They bring spirit to life.

A WOW factor workplace is one where customers experience that WOW spirit time and time again. Once they experience that WOW spirit, they come to expect that WOW spirit, and they rely on that WOW spirit at every touch point. In a real WOW factor workplace, customers are rarely disappointed because the team members working there love what they do, and their passion shows. It's evident to everyone.

Life is too short to not spend your days doing something you love, something which inspires you, something you might even be willing to do for free if you had some way to pay the bills.

Whenever I have the opportunity to interact with an organization I love to do business with, it's usually because the staff makes me feel special, like a VIP. Often, when that organization makes me feel like a Very Important Person, it's usually due to employees who, when asked, unashamedly say they love their job, and they love their boss. There is a beautiful spiral of spirit.

Here's another example:

I originally came to know Donald Stamets, now General Manager for the Flagship Solage—an Auberge Resort located in Napa Valley, California, thanks to a whole series of WOW experiences I had at each of the previous resorts he had managed for well over a decade, from California to Florida. One of those resorts, The Resort at Pelican Hill, was voted "Top US Resort" by *Conde Nast Traveler* readers.

Donald shared this with me:

> I think it's important you love what you do. I'm not exposed to every industry out there, but certainly hospitality has got to be a very difficult one because you're dealing with people. Most industries do deal with people, but we are a customer-based organization. We've got 98,000 interaction possibilities a year with customers checking in and checking out.
>
> There's a quote in the hotel business: "You're only as good as your last checkout."
>
> You just must stay positive and love what you do.
>
> When I drive up to this resort every day, I still get butterflies in my stomach. I say, "This is my kingdom." I feel like the mayor. I want amazing, amazing community. You've got to love what you do, and if you don't, then you're not in the right business.

Back when I lived in Southern California, I attended and hosted several lovely business events at each of the two resorts Donald managed there, the Island Hotel and the Resort at Pelican Hill. No event was ever what one might consider inexpensive, but every single one was spectacular, carried off with aplomb, and worth every penny. I was well aware that the staff who reported to Donald from both resorts loved him.

When planning a big milestone birthday celebration for my dad shortly after moving to Florida, I immediately selected the local Omni Resort for hosting this special event due to the fact the Omni had just announced the arrival of their new general manager, Donald Stamets.

Familiar with Donald's ethos and his former teams' attention to every detail, I fully expected the Omni's Sunrise Café would be classy, yet comfortable and homey, and the staff would be gracious, warm, and charmingly friendly. I knew if anyone could help me pull off a perfect surprise birthday breakfast for my dad, it would be a team reporting to Donald.

Upon our arrival on the morning of the event, the hostess greeted us warmly and immediately escorted us to a lovely table for four, right in front of a huge picture window which offered an extraordinary view of the ocean. As soon as we sat down, my dad leaned across the table and said, "THIS is nice. Now we need a Bloody Mary!"

He obviously hadn't noticed a second hostess standing right next to him with a tray of Bloody Marys. I smiled and tipped my head toward the hostess, who then placed a Bloody Mary in front of Dad, saying, "Here's to the Birthday Boy."

Dad was in heaven, and Mom was blown away. I smiled again and said, "What would you expect? It IS your birthday."

Just then Miss Donnie, a most charming and jovial breakfast chef, came out of the kitchen and walked directly to our table to wish Dad a great big Happy Birthday, exclaiming in her charming southern drawl, "I have some mighty good food just waiting for you in the kitchen. If you would like to come with me, I'll show you the kitchen and make you a real special omelet. We have lots of other good things in there I've made myself."

We couldn't resist that invitation, so we all got up and followed Miss Donnie for a personally guided tour of the sparkling, shiny white subway-tiled buffet kitchen. It was indeed a feast for the eyes.

After taking in the amazingly beautiful display of freshly baked breads and pastries, mountains of colorful fresh fruits, vast assortments of meats and cheeses and more, my dad noticed no one else was at the omelet bar, so he whispered to Miss Donnie, "I'd like one of those special omelets of yours." She proudly said, "Okay, you just tell me what you like, and I'll make you my very best omelet ever!" It was apparent she couldn't wait to start cooking up a feast for the King of the Day.

While watching Miss Donnie whip up this best-ever concoction, I asked her my favorite interview question: "How long have you worked here?"

Miss Donnie's eyes twinkled as she tilted her head, silently recalling her many fond memories, and replied, "Oh my. It's been years and years. My family keeps telling me it's time to retire, and I suppose it is, but I'm just having too much fun working here, being around nice folks like you. Why on earth would I want to retire? Maybe next year, but not any time soon."

Clearly, Miss Donnie cherished every one of those many important and special workdays she held so dearly in her memory. Her joy and love for her profession extended to everyone around her. You couldn't help but feel it.

At that instant, a delightful two-person band playing the guitar and a bass somehow magically started to play an assortment of Dad's favorite songs from the seventies, including "Here Comes the Sun." Dad smiled big as he exclaimed, "Oh, I love that song!"

> **The only way to do great work is to love what you do. If you haven't found it yet, keep looking. Don't settle.**
> —Steve Jobs, Chairman, CEO and a Cofounder of Apple, Inc.

A while later, as Dad devoured his second plate of hot food (this time Miss Donnie's homemade biscuits and gravy), Miss Donnie once again magically reappeared at our table to ask, "Well, whadda y'all think?"

It was as though we were the only guests in the place, and Miss Donnie had nothing more important to do than ensure my dad had the birthday celebration of a lifetime.

When it finally came time to leave, Dad stood up to help my mom from her chair. Mom said reluctantly, "Oh, do we have to leave? I want to spend the afternoon here. This is so nice." With that, Mom leaned over to me and suggested, "Let's do this again."

I could now go on and on telling you about several more WOW factor experiences we had many times at the Omni Resort after Donald Stamets came on board, but you probably get the idea. Donald is one WOW factor workplace leader who loves what he does, as does virtually every member of his team.

By now, you may be wondering just how any organization can continuously create one extraordinary experience after another, again and again. Clearly, these workplaces are comprised largely of employees who love their jobs. But what is the magic behind the rampant employee engagement that brings such WOW factor splendor to reality?

For the remainder of this book, we will peel back the onion, so to speak, to uncover how Best Places to Work and their WOW factor workplace leaders ignite such spirit in the hearts and minds of their employees, peers, and audiences. I'll even throw in some of my own stories along the way.

Now serving as the Program Director of Healthcare Management in the Jindal School of Management at the University of Texas-Dallas, Britt Berrett has been widely recognized for his commitment to teams and organizational culture.

Britt came to my attention as a WOW factor workplace best-ever boss when he was President of Texas Health Presbyterian Hospital-Dallas. Britt's organization had been awarded "The Best Place to Work" award by the *Dallas Business Journal,* and they were also honored as one of the "Top 50 Best Places to Work in the State of Texas."

When I asked him, "What is the key to employee engagement?" Britt replied:

> Purpose and Meaning. That, for me, is the key. To do what you do with purpose and meaning. It's profoundly important to you, personally. We need meaning.

I know when I get exhausted at the end of the day I'll go to the lobby. I'll sit in the lobby in one of those chairs. I'll watch the patients walk in and out. They are scared. They don't know what to do. They're going to be entering a new environment. We'll take their clothes. We'll poke and prod them all night long. If I, as a leader, can understand my role in blessing their lives, if it can give me purpose and meaning, then I'll get up earlier, stay later, and be much more purposeful in my efforts. That's invigorating.

I hope others see that because the "nine-to-five" is gone. I think the "nine-to-five" is doomed in any organization that doesn't have an engaged team that loves what they do. They find the meaning behind it. It doesn't have to be just in health care. It can be in IT. It can be in law enforcement. It can be in education. You can feel someone who is genuine. You can absolutely feel the love.

One friend described it as, "You are so excited about the subject you're literally spitting your words." You're not just talking; you're really engaging. When you are in that environment, those with whom we work get it. They feel it. There's a spirit associated with it which is powerful.

Too often, we are fearful of opening ourselves up to that, because once you open yourself up to that passion, there are tragedies, there are disappointments, there's the corporation, there are staff members who fail you. It can be hurtful. That's why you must cowboy up, as we say here in Texas, and get back in the game. Get back in the game with meaning. That's what I've seen. I've seen it time and time again. Getting back in and doing so with purpose.

As it relates to those who have never really cared about the team—that is just not how they're wired—you've got to figure it out. You've got to reset the clock. Yours will be a hollow profession. You will hit a midlife crisis, and it will blow your mind.

I grieve for individuals who come to my office and say, "I've been in this industry for decades, and I hate it. I want to get into another industry. I want to do a big midlife career change." I grieve for the decades they've spent in a profession they haven't liked. Some postpone it because the money's good.

I gave up my entire retirement to join this faith-based organization. I asked myself, "What's important in life?" Sometimes you've just got to do that. You have just got to make the hard decision because it's not going to get any easier in the future. You're not going to suddenly **The great ones found the passion.** wake up and go, "Man, I've hated my job for the last decade, but now I like it." It doesn't work that way. It gets worse.

Sometimes you must make the tough decision. If you've behaved in a way that's been uncaring and unfeeling, you need to do, as they say, a checkup from the neck up. You've got to figure that out. Find meaning and purpose in your life and then pursue that.

It's interesting for me to see the new health care providers. There was a group who got into medicine because they thought they could make a lot of money. That's the only reason they got in. Today, with health care reform, they are some of the most dissatisfied, disgruntled, and angry. One said to me, "You know, I'm sick and tired of being sick and tired." It's true.

The great ones found the passion. They weren't chasing after the dollars. Their intent was not to make a lot of money and drive the fancy car. Do they want a good lifestyle? Sure. But they felt the passion and purpose in health care. That's helped them navigate through the white waters of change. The same would be true for any industry. Find the meaning behind it.

When I interjected with, "What is the secret to success in driving innovation?" Britt said:

One of my great mentors was my father, but he was a different kind of leader. It was a different era. The lumber industry. They made the shingles ... boom, boom, boom ... very, very structured and objective. There wasn't much innovation in that space, so he was a transactional leader. A good man, a loving father, but in his business life, he hit the golden age, and his brain exploded. He just said, "What's it all about?"

He had this life change of "What's it all about?" and changed his career. He went into a field he loved. For me, it was fascinating to watch.

I asked, "Dad, what are some of your great regrets?"

He said, "Every place I've been, when I left, it failed miserably. I always grieved over that."

 "Why do you think that happened?"

"Because I never trained them. I never allowed them to make decisions for themselves. Everything came through me. I was in charge, and they did as I said. I've got a strong personality, and I never built a team."

I've thought a lot about that over the years. I recognized that when you have a static environment, when the business doesn't change, and that's how you approach it, you are doomed to failure.

How many shingles are made today? The mills he ran are closed. He didn't shift the organization to be nimble. When he didn't have the idea, he certainly didn't let any of his team members have the idea. Could he have shifted? Sure. There are plenty of wood products out there. Could he have done something differently? Absolutely. However, he didn't allow the team to do that. The dilemma he faced was that he removed himself from that profession.

Then he got it. He started building amazing teams. I watched as he was in a different profession and area, and how he inspired individuals. It was a wake-up call for me on how he never looked back at his time in the lumber industry with fondness. But at the age of fifty and until his passing, he was energized.

I think that approach creates innovation, responsiveness to change. I think he probably would have been in the same industry until the day he died if he would have allowed others to be innovative and creative.

Dr. Mark Goulston interviewed WOW factor workplace leader, Paul Spiegelman, Founder of BerylHealth, and the Beryl Institute. Paul also cofounded the Small Giants Community, an organization which brings values-based leaders together. These days Paul focuses his efforts on the Small Giants Community.

While Paul was CEO of BerylHealth, he led a unique people-centric culture for a company which won nine "Best Place to Work" awards. As if that isn't impressive enough, BerylHealth was also voted the #2 "Best Medium-Sized Company to Work for in America."

Paul himself was honored with the Ernst & Young "Entrepreneur of the Year" award in 2010. He shared this insight with us:

I've never looked at myself as an entrepreneur, really, because I always thought of the entrepreneur as that ambitious person who built something, sold it, bought something else, grew it, sold it, and did that multiple times.

I don't want to be paid because I love what I do.

I've had one gig my whole life. The term which resonated with me, one a mentor told me about a while ago, was this idea of "success and significance." We can achieve success, depending on what that means to you. It might be money or achieving some level of wealth. But how does that feel in the end? How do we sustain a feeling or maintain our business? It's all very personal.

For me, "significance" became the impact I could have on other people. The importance of making more money, for me, went out a long time ago. It wasn't about making more money.

I sold my company for a lot of money and yet I took a job with another company, the company that bought us. I said, "I don't want to be paid." I don't want to be paid because I love what I do. I'm going to feel best about touching other people's lives and, hopefully, helping other leaders grow their businesses.

I think as I've grown, as I've gotten older, I've started to think about meaning in my life. What's most important? I realized that note I'd get from someone, that handwritten note card I would get from an employee that said: "Thank you. You've changed my life. This is the best place I've ever worked" or "You've taught me something I would never have learned" is much more powerful, much more valuable than any amount of money I could have in the bank. That money sits there and is going to make my children comfortable and give them opportunities. But that's not going to be what makes me ultimately happy in my life.

It's how many people I can touch with the message to show having this set of values, caring about people and paying it forward, that drives the true happiness in my heart.

Dr. Mark asked Paul, "Do you think loyalty is important, or is it okay to have disloyal employees who stay there only as long as you reward them with money?"

Paul replied:

I was able to see that in my own business. We created tremendous loyalty. We were in a call center industry that's known for over 100% attrition, where nobody would stay around. It's a boiler room operation, a commodity business that competes on cost— a low-margin, high-attrition business.

Still, we turned it into a kind of business that won nine awards as a "Best Place to Work" company. We were the Number Two "Best Place to Work in America." We were five to six times more profitable than other companies in our industry. We did that by merely caring for our employees in the totality of their lives, having attrition at a fraction of what you'd see in a typical call center-type business.

These were single moms who were working for that paycheck every couple of weeks. Yet, if we gave them a great environment, if we let them have some fun, if we showed we cared about them when they had an event in their life that was important to them (a birth, a death), if we helped them and showed we were interested in them as a person, they would do anything for us. It created tremendous loyalty. They worked harder, and it did more for our business.

We were a premium provider who charged 30% to 40% more than our next closest competitor. How did we do that in a commodity-type business? Our customers not only were willing to pay that, but they valued the culture we created because it meant something to them. They knew we were going to be doing a better job for them.

What's interesting, and I can't get my arms around, is why leaders don't see this connection. Why financials tend to drive decision-making, versus putting people first, letting that drive customer loyalty, letting that drive profit. It's something I called over the years, "the circle of growth." If we focus first and foremost on people, that's going to drive customer loyalty. It's going to drive profit that we'll invest back in our people, giving them better tools and resources to do their jobs.

If you ask about the *Inc.* readers or *Fast Company,* I would say there are a portion of those people would get this message. Others are more ambitious: "I want to make the *Inc. 5000* list of the fastest growing companies in America" or "I want to develop the next app for the iPhone and make a billion dollars." There are still a lot of people out there who are like that. That's okay. They're going to have great inventions, and they're going to advance the world.

However, I think what you're seeing, over the next ten to twenty years, is that the methodology of how to create a successful and sustainable business is going to change completely. I think the old ways of command and control—I tell you what to do instead of I tell you why you're doing it and empower you to make decisions and allow you to fail—I think that's going to change completely. We need more data to support this, but I think you're starting to see this over time.

Talk about some of the companies like Costco, Whole Foods, the Container Store, Southwest Airlines. What's common among these companies? It's a multi-stakeholder approach to business where employees come first. If you look at their data, they're far more profitable than other companies in their industries. The key is, why can't we move more quickly and get other people to see the light?

Good question.

Speaking of Southwest Airlines, let's look at them now. As a carrier which enjoys giving 100+ million customers a year the *freedom to fly*, Southwest Airlines has had some pretty impressive results, despite being in an industry noted for razor-thin profit margins.

Unlike most air carriers, Southwest has consistently received the lowest ratio of complaints per passengers boarded of all major US carriers that have been reporting statistics to the Department of Transportation (DOT) since September 1987, which is when the DOT began tracking Customer Satisfaction statistics and publishing its Air Travel Consumer Report. Since 2014, Southwest has carried the most domestic passengers of any US airline.

Southwest was rated by J.D. Power as the USA's best airline for 2017 and 2018. Scoring 818 points on a 1,000-point scale in J.D. Power's survey of individual airline ratings for 2018, Southwest scored the highest in both J.D. Power's "Low-Cost Carrier" category *and* among ALL carriers surveyed. That, in and of itself, is a WOW!

A while back, I had the wonderful opportunity to speak with then-Senior Vice President of Customers for Southwest Airlines, the late Teresa Laraba, one of the highest-ranking female executives in the airline industry. Until her passing on Christmas day 2015, Teresa provided senior leadership for three departments: Customer Support & Services, Customer Relations & Rapid Rewards, and Customer Services. She ensured the airline's many customer-focused activities were coordinated and aligned to one vision for how Southwest would continue to meet its customers' current and future needs better.

Teresa shared this story with me:

I have always been viewed as—jokingly—Mother Teresa (with the first name Teresa), at home and work and even early on in my jobs, even as a kid, working and waiting on tables, coaching swimming lessons, and coaching the swim team. I always got so much joy out of watching everybody else succeed (not putting together what a difference that was going to make in my life). It was just whom I had become.

I celebrated so much watching everybody else succeed. It would just hurt me when the kids didn't succeed. It tapped into a side of me that I knew if I could make sure other people were successful, or be there for them when they weren't, that fed me.

So, I wound up at Southwest Airlines. It almost was as if Southwest Airlines was made for me. It was a company that allowed you to be that way. Over the thirty years I've been here, I've had so many opportunities to see what a difference it makes to work for a company that lets you care.

I have worked for some leaders at Southwest Airlines who were not that way. I have watched some of them come and go as a result of the fact they didn't know how to put people first. Or they tried, and it was so unnatural it wasn't sustainable.

If you put other people first, if you are willing to do what they are doing, walk a mile in their shoes, stand next to the employees and do everything you ask anybody else to do, they will do anything for you.

My very first leader, at the time, was in an airport environment and he ran the station. I didn't know much about Southwest when I started. I was young; I was twenty-one. It was a great job. I was going to be a customer service agent, working with the public. I thought this would be great. I wasn't aware of what the core values were of Southwest when I first got here.

Working with him was quite an experience. He was very gruff, very improper in the sense the language he used was colorful. It was back in the early eighties then, so maybe not as concerning to some as it would be now. He led with "You do what I tell you. You don't ask any questions. We've got an airline to run. Get these planes out on time."

On one side, that's exactly what we were there to do. We were there to run an airline, to get airplanes out. But there were so many other people, and even my supervisors who reported to him weren't like him. I started to realize you didn't have to be gruff to get people to do their job. Still, that's how he managed.

When he managed that way, it was interesting to watch how people, and even myself, responded to him. You almost bury some of the caring you have, to meet their leadership style. It causes conflict. So, although I was young, I knew at the end of the day, I was going to struggle with working with somebody who had that type of approach.

We worked together for a couple of years, and then he moved on to another location, and we got another new leader who was a much better blend of heart and profession. That was when I really had a chance to tap even more into the fact if you show people you care, if you put other people first, if you are willing to do what they are doing, walk a mile in their shoes, stand next to the employees and do everything you ask anybody else to do, they will do anything for you.

That was when I started to grow into understanding how I was raised and, because I was the type of person who cares, there was a place for that in the workforce. It wasn't something you had to stifle or hide because it was inappropriate. You just had to use it the right ways.

I was attracted to Southwest Airlines. I'd flown as a college student between Dallas and Lubbock. My grandmother had passed away when we first moved to El Paso. My mom and dad and I flew on Southwest to get to Dallas for her funeral. It wasn't a full airplane, but I was so moved by how fun everybody was. Here we were, having a tough time, and the flight attendants were caring. They were asking my mom and dad if they were okay. You could feel a difference. You could feel they were engaging in a way I don't think I would have picked up on otherwise.

Every time I had an opportunity to fly, it resonated with me. I did know Southwest Airlines was known as a company that hired fun people. It was a young and up-and-coming company. It looked for employees who enjoyed the customer and who enjoyed the interaction with the public. That's what drew me in first.

The opportunity then to promote into leadership is what has kept me here because it has given me a chance to make a difference in people's lives, not just personally but professionally. That has fed something I can't seem to step away from.

We're lucky at Southwest. We first try to hire people who care. Our hiring process is looking for people who genuinely enjoy what they do. We call it the Servant's Heart. People who have a Servant's Heart are people who, especially if you're going to be on the service side of it, enjoy serving. Not somebody who merely pretends they enjoy serving.

We look for kindhearted people as we go through the interview process. It could be anywhere from how you dealt with the agent when they put you on the airplane, to the shuttle driver, to the hotel front desk. If we get a report telling us an employee or a prospective employee hasn't been kind to somebody, that makes a difference for us. We won't hire that somebody. We've already set ourselves up to look for people who care.

We're also, now, a company of forty-five-thousand employees, and we're going to get employees who are qualified at what we need and have a caring attitude when we interview them.

On a similar note, Teresa shared this about loving what you do and being loved in return:

I don't like to talk about myself, but I save every little thank you note I get. I keep the notes I get back from people when I was doing what I thought we were supposed to do, what I knew I should do, and how it touched somebody. I keep those to remind me it's been worth the effort.

If you don't love your workplace, if you are not energized and fulfilled by your role, you owe it to yourself and those around you to make a change.

I know I've made a difference in people's lives when they've gone through some rough things because I have been able to share when I have, when I've been able to reach out and be somebody else's support, either losing a family member or breast cancer. Not because it gave me attention, but because it gave that person comfort. I think if you do it, and I know I do it because somebody has done it for me, and I know how good that felt, I can't help but to want to pay it forward.

I'm fortunate in the fact I have two daughters who are very much like me, in that sense, and who are already seeing the value in doing that in living their lives that way.

That, my friend, is what they call "The Southwest Spirit." That's also the spirit of a WOW factor workplace.

Soundbite FROM DR. MARK

People who focus on "getting and having more" often end up unhappy at the end of their lives, whereas people who focus on "giving and caring more" usually end up happy.

ACTION STEPS

1 Think about your best-ever workplace experience (paid or unpaid).

- What was your role?
- How did people treat each other?
- How did the team members behave in general?
- What was the overall level of performance?
- Were there goals for the entire organization/your department/your own goals? Who defined them?
- How loyal were the employees?
- How loyal were the lower-level and mid-level managers?
- How loyal were the customers/clients/patients/patrons/donors?

FOUR

Envision WOW Together

You must have a vision and you must be able to sell that vision.
The people who work for you must be part of that vision.
—REINHOLD PREIK
Founder and CEO Emeritus of Chemcraft International

The people around us want to be inspired. To inspire them, they need to see an outcome which is in their best interest, one which helps them achieve their own goals. They need to understand, "What's in it for me?" When your team members, peers, and superiors fully understand what you are trying to accomplish and how that works right in line with what they are trying to accomplish, it will be far easier for you to work together toward a common goal. It's crucial if you intend to create and ultimately achieve a WOW vision.

Certainly, we all like to feel our work makes a difference and is noticed, whether we are working on something routine or magnificent. Successful leaders, especially heartfelt leaders, make sure the people working above, for, and with them know they and their contributions are appreciated, especially if they are expected to go above and beyond the normal call of duty to make that WOW vision a reality. Sometimes a simple "thank you" can have more power than you'd think. Giving meaningful credit, when credit is due, can pay compounded dividends.

It's not unusual these days to be faced with a deadline which seems impossible to meet. Some people faced with an unrealistic deadline may complain, drag their feet, give up, or thwart the effort. Rather than allow anyone to take a defeatist's attitude, use whatever sense of urgency can be created by the deadline to gain focus and needed support.

Looming deadlines can sometimes make it easier to prioritize tasks, weed out the less important things which can wait until later, and maybe even eliminate routine tasks which perhaps don't need to be done at all. As I told my staff, "Don't ever let a good crisis go to waste."

Having spent years working in global bureaucracies, I found it could sometimes be challenging to get anything of real consequence done until there was a pending crisis. I loved to leverage a crisis situation because that was when I was able to present big, bold, audacious ideas to conquer the looming giant…*et voilà*…that's when I could magically get funding and headcount (which was otherwise impossible to get), all because the CEO was finally convinced we had an impossible deadline and failure would not be in his best interest. Rather than shrink from leading an "impossible" effort, I'd usually be the one to step up to the crisis plate with a plan.

Now, this doesn't mean I would be foolhardy. It doesn't mean I would be willing to take on an absurd project which wasn't appropriately resourced. It means I'd first gather a small team of experts from wherever I could find them. Together we—my band of experts and I—would come up with a potential solution. Together we would determine what it would require in terms of staffing

> **Attitude is everything. Pick a good one.**

and pinpoint where to go to find and acquire the resources. Next, we would share the vision with those resources and invite them to join our effort. This would usually get a buzz humming from the bottom up.

I discovered early on that people want to work with others who exude a "can-do" attitude, demonstrate the knowledge and confidence to create success, possess a reputation for getting things done (while making it fun in the process), and willingly share the limelight. Once people know what's in it for them, big, bold plans can quickly inspire volunteers to eagerly jump on board to bring those WOW ideas to life.

For many years I had a brightly colored sign hanging on the wall behind my desk which said: "Attitude is everything. Pick a good one." Conveying an "I'm confident we can do this" attitude and message is sometimes all that's needed to generate the traction, the talent, the ideas, and ultimately the funding necessary to make WOW a reality.

Somewhere in the middle of my career, my organization was focused on designing supply chain management process solutions and information services for design engineers and component engineers in high-tech manufacturing firms. Circumstances propelled me to become a noted expert on international law and regulations impacting global high-tech manufacturers. As a result, I traveled extensively to meet with the CEOs, VPs of engineering, VPs of manufacturing and chief operating officers (COOs) of major manufacturers which maintained manufacturing operations in Europe, Mexico, and Asia. The Fortune 200 company I worked for at the time, Arrow Electronics, supplied electronic components to their global operations.

Seemingly out of the blue, the government of China announced it would be instituting new regulations to restrict the use of hazardous substances in electronic components for products manufactured in China. Moreover, China would require new labeling on all electronic technology packaging entering the country. Within six months, all electronic components to be shipped into China (for the manufacture of end products, which would ultimately be exported out of China) would be stopped at the border and prevented from delivery to manufacturing sites within China if not properly labeled with all the substances used in the manufacture of the components.

This portended to be a much more significant challenge than simply relabeling our component packaging. Worse yet, our company's inability to meet the new import/export labeling requirements could potentially mean hundreds of millions of dollars' worth of products might be turned away at the border. Furthermore, our high-tech manufacturing customers could be out billions of dollars in finished goods which could not be shipped out of China to their end customers throughout the rest of the world. Not meeting the pending Chinese regulations could have consequences of almost unimaginable magnitude worldwide.

For several months before this, I had been keeping our Chief Compliance Officer and CEO abreast of the rumors China might be planning to take such action. I had reason to believe it wasn't just a rumor, based on information I obtained while attending international supply chain conferences where foreign dignitaries and technology experts from around the world would gather to discuss such things.

As a global electronic components distributor, complying with such regulations would impact the core of our business operations, our database management systems, our product labeling processes, and our shipping procedures, not to mention the fact that several distribution hubs we ran around the world utilized different systems and procedures in various countries. Changing all of them would be a tremendous undertaking.

On the other hand, the implications of such legal restrictions being imposed by China seemed so outlandish, most high-tech CEOs, including ours, believed it would never really happen. Most believed it was just an empty threat and saber-rattling.

Just give it a rest, and this will all go away.

For a while, my warnings to our executive management team were treated as though they had come straight out of the children's book *Chicken Little* …The sky is falling … the sky is falling … . Their response was something akin to "Don't worry about it."

Then it happened. China formally announced the rest of the world would have just six months to comply with what seemed to be, by anyone who had not already started working on a solution, a completely unrealistic deadline. Even then, it took a few more weeks to get an opportunity to update our chief executives.

When I finally did, their response was, "The whole idea will certainly be called off by the Chinese government. Even China can't create and institute such onerous border inspection processes to manage the huge volumes of product crossing their borders in such a ridiculously short timeframe. Just give it a rest, and this will all go away."

Not believing China had any intention of calling off or even postponing the new regulations, I personally contacted every relevant internal senior leader in each country where we had operations that could potentially be impacted. I asked them to dedicate staff to work with me in the (hopefully) unlikely event we had to meet a now-increasingly-closer deadline.

It certainly helped to be known throughout the company as *the* expert on the topic. As a result, within a relatively short time, I had commitments from virtually every person in the company globally who needed to be involved in implementing a solution should my concerns become a reality.

I immediately instituted weekly conference calls in which nearly 100 individuals participated … not an easy task, given all the time zones to consider. Fortunately, people were unusually flexible and eager to be part of such a vast undertaking. Some of our best and brightest people, in country after country, stepped up to the plate. We educated each other as needed. Certainly, none of us alone had the expertise or wherewithal to map out a solution as complex as we required to address this challenge. We prepared our SWAT team to jump into action as soon as the call to activate arrived from on high.

Eventually that day came.

We were down to little more than three months to D-Day when several of our customers' CEOs started calling our CEO, demanding to know what our plan was.

Thank goodness we had a plan.

The implementation timeframe was now unreasonably shorter than ever—seemingly impossibly—but we had no choice. We had to jump into action to meet the deadline. No other projects mattered.

The CEO announced I could have whatever staff I needed dedicated to the project. We would fly the key country team leaders in from around the world by the following Monday to get the project kick-started. Our Chief Compliance Officer would be our project sponsor. I would update him weekly and would have immediate access to him at any time when needed.

I required many on the team to attend conference calls at 11 p.m. or 5 a.m., depending on where they were based in the world. I was quite amazed at how optimistic (albeit scared) everyone was. If anything got in our way, I would immediately go to the Chief Compliance Officer. When necessary, he would go to the CEO, and we would then quickly get what we needed.

To make a long story short, we designed and implemented new global databases along with new shipping and labeling processes with just days to spare.

Then we waited, counting the hours until D-Day. Would China let our shipments in? Would they all pass inspection? As the clock clicked down to the deadline, we held our breath and readied to implement any needed fail-safe plans.

Midnight of D-Day sounded in Hong Kong. Even our legal teams watched their monitors for the first reports back from our Hong Kong office to confirm whether the first shipments were accepted or returned.

They went through.

I believe you could have heard the exuberant cheering from our New York headquarters all the way to Beijing. Of course, that "All Clear" message was related to just one Chinese border station. Would our shipments be accepted at other Chinese ports of entry? Again, we waited ... and waited.

Finally, Hong Kong called with a thumbs-up. We had done the seemingly impossible.

Every member of the team had given it their personal best. Virtually every member of the team had maintained a positive can-do attitude the entire time (those few who didn't were quickly removed from the group). It required every member we had on the team to pull off such a vast WOW project. Our customers were incredibly grateful, and we were rewarded for it with even more of their business in the following months.

My next task was to plan a huge thank you celebration. After all we had been through, implementing that part was a piece of cake ... but it was one final, very crucial step if we were to be successful the next time such an enormous challenge presented itself. In the end, we were a closer team and a better company for it. We were now, at least for this moment, unstoppable. WOW!

Of course, not every WOW mission should be focused on averting a crisis. Yet, it is crucial to have an overarching intention always to be the best at whatever you do.

While interviewing several members of the senior leadership team at Southwest Airlines, I had the opportunity to speak with Colleen Barrett, president emeritus and corporate secretary. Colleen was there in the earliest days, alongside Southwest Airlines' cofounder and former Chairman and CEO, Herb Kelleher, who passed away in 2019 at the age of 87. Colleen shared this about Herb Kelleher's earliest WOW vision for Southwest:

> **We believe an organization will stand out only if it is willing to take on seemingly impossible tasks.**
> —Thomas J. Watson, Jr., 2nd President of IBM, Chairman and CEO during IBM's most explosive period of growth.

The only legacy, really, Herb ever wanted to leave, was a legacy for his kids and his grandkids and for all our employees' kids and grandkids.

He never had a goal to be the biggest. He never had a goal to be the most profitable. What he did want: he wanted to be the best. He wanted to be the best in terms of employee culture. And he wanted to be the best in terms of customer service and delivery.

That was a dream of his. It wasn't to be rich. You know, money has never really meant anything to him personally, or he'd still be practicing law. He could have made ten times more money.

Southwest was a cause. It was a mission. It was a cause for him. And it is for most, at least.

Teresa Laraba, whom I introduced you to in the previous chapter, provided a bit more insight into the implementation of the Southwest mission to be the best at employee culture, customer service, and delivery:

> Early on, when we started, one of the taglines was: *Somebody up here loves you.* We used the word *love* in a space where it had not been used, especially in the airline industry. Our stock symbol is LUV. We were open about introducing love to corporate America and the airline industry. We were going to have a product which loved you and a company which was going to serve you and appreciate you doing business with us versus the attitude: "You exist to keep us in business."
>
> Very early on, the customer became Number One. The difference that was going to set us apart was going to be our people. It was going to be how our people deliver on that promise, which meant how our flight attendants interacted with our customers, how our airport employees interacted with our customers. We encouraged people from day one to be themselves.
>
> The silliness you see on Southwest, the jokes and some of the singing of the emergency announcements, all that does is continue to retrench in the airline industry you can still be different, you can still care, you can still provide a fun experience for customers, especially in an industry which has not been so fun.
>
> After 9/11, we purposely took some humor out. We did not want our flight attendants to get back on those airplanes right away and start making jokes and doing things we've done before. We had to take a little bit of a breather. Everybody had to, not be buttoned up, not be uncaring, but be sensitive to what the public was experiencing.
>
> It didn't take long before our customers were saying, "I miss that." You knew, quickly, you needed to bring that back. However, we never took away the fact we cared. We just had

to be aware of the fact the industry had changed. There was a sensitive time for the public, and we needed to be sensitive to how we were going to respond to that.

We have never lacked from feedback from our customers. I call them "Southwest Evangelists." We have customers who, I think, we should pay to work for us because they are so committed to our brand. We started to hear from them via e-mail and via letters: a) they were glad we were still in the air, and b) they looked forward to getting on a Southwest plane. "I look forward to the jokes and the songs and the things Southwest brought." It gave you a sense that things were going to be okay, and we would get back to normal.

When our customers are asking us to bring it back, and they're saying it to our flight attendants, that's when you know you have the right—and really, the responsibility—to bring back something you stepped away from for a short while. Customers will definitely let you know. And they did ... loud and clear.

It's time for you to meet another best-ever boss, Reinhold Preik, the retired founder and CEO emeritus of Chemcraft International. Chemcraft is one of the most successful private manufacturers of innovative specialty coatings in North America. These days, he focuses his energies on his charitable foundation and giving to others.

Rein was born in East Germany before World War II. After the war, he emigrated to Canada and eventually founded Chemcraft. His incredible journey was documented in his autobiography, *My Moments in Time: A Journey from Poverty to Destiny.* Some of the leaders who reported to Rein at Chemcraft have stayed with Rein throughout their careers. Diana Hyunen, former chief financial officer at Chemcraft, still works with him to this day. In Rein's autobiography, Diana described him this way:

Rein was like a general, standing at the forefront to forge ahead and make ideas happen. Over the years, we worked on organic growth, but one of his goals was to become global. He started in Ontario, Canada. He led the acquisition of the American companies and then gained representation in Europe, Singapore, and Brazil. It was continually evolving.

Rein is an incredible visionary to start with something so small and to have the focus to grow a company into something of which we are all very proud. He does that with everything he is part of.

In 2007, Rein decided to consider selling the company for several different reasons. I think it was difficult for him because he was extremely loyal to and protective of all his employees. Some of the biggest chemical companies in the world wanted to buy it, but he was careful because although he knew it was time to sell, he wanted to create a legacy.

Rein shared this with me about selling a vision:

The way I see it, it's a matter of selling. If you are a public company, you've got to be able to sell your shareholders—or partners, or whatever you have—on the vision, and the idea that the vision you have will eventually return value. If you don't have a vision, you are just plodding along, you only want a little return this year and only as much next year as we have this year, that's quite different.

Unfortunately, when you become a huge company, it gets tough to operate on the Vision Principle because you are already filling up so much space in the industry. That's why you see so many mergers ... because they don't know where to go. Somebody says, "We can increase our value by merging with this other company. We can get rid of a whole bunch of people, and our bottom line will look better."

The only alternative you have is to be an innovator. If you are going to be an innovator, you must have a vision and you must be able to sell that vision. The people who work for you must be part of that vision.

While conducting our research, another WOW factor workplace best-ever boss was referred to us, Tim Hindes, CEO of Stay Metrics. Tim started as a truck driver and dispatcher. Tim transitioned to management early in his trucking career. He eventually became a highly successful serial entrepreneur known for his passion for creating cultures which put the wants and needs of employees at the forefront.

Tim and his business partner teamed up with top researchers in behavioral psychology, management, and organizational culture. Their goal was to create a rewards and recognition platform that would promote a better culture and work experience for drivers in the trucking industry.

Tim shared this about the way he and his business partner envisioned WOW:

> Our mantra is when somebody comes to work for us for a period of time, and if somebody like yourself comes in and says, "How do you like working for Tim Hindes?", if the answer isn't "This is the absolute best place I've ever worked in my life... they treat me so much better here than I've ever been treated in my life," we fail.
>
> **We want to take this on steroids to the point we want to do things for our employees nobody else does.**
>
> If the answer is, "Yeah, it's okay. It's a pretty good place to work," then we totally fail.
>
> We want to take this on steroids to the point we want to do things for our employees nobody else does.

Recall my personal story from the last chapter about the WOW factor experiences I had with the various resort hotel teams led by Donald Stamets, now general manager for Solage, an Auberge resort in Calistoga, CA. Donald began his hospitality career right after college with the Westin Bonaventure Hotel in Los Angeles. Donald shared this example of how he and his teams envision WOW together:

> I've always had a gift to walk into a room and take command of that room, for whatever reason. I think it's because I exude this positivity. I'm very conscious of body language and wanting to go up to be "aggressively hospitable" to others. It's something I like to teach here in the hotel: Aggressive Hospitality.
>
> These almost sound like antonyms of each other because you've got to be aggressive and you've got to be hospitable. It's about going up and making sure you can greet people and give them something they need before they know they need it. It's essential in the hospitality world.
>
> There's a "pyramid" I teach in orientation that I just did in a class today. Imagine a pyramid with levels showing *Expected, Requested,* and *Delighted.* I ask the orientation crowd, "When people come to a resort of this caliber, what are some of the things they expect?"
>
> "An ocean view."
>
> "A pool."
>
> "A smile."
>
> "Someone to open the door for you."
>
> "Food and beverage options."
>
> There are a thousand answers, none of which are wrong, of course.

I say, "Okay. If we're able to give customers everything they expect, is that good enough?"

Some people say, "Yeah! That's great!"

I say, "Absolutely not. We've failed. If people expect it, and we're just giving them what they expect, that's nothing. Right?"

Then the light bulb starts to go on with a few people in the room, which is exciting to watch. Then we jump up to the next tier, which is Requested.

I say, "Now the customers are here, and they start requesting things: high floor, king bed, close to the elevator, pet friendly, away from the elevator, close to the Conference Center, ocean view, corner suite, margarita-on-the-rocks, hamburger medium rare, an extra rollaway, extra towels."

Then I say, "Okay. Now we deliver all those things. Is that good enough?"

"Oh, yeah. That's great!"

"No! We're an epic failure if we can only deliver to the customers what they ask for. They are paying us. Certainly we should give them what they're asking for. But we're in the hospitality business. Our job is to push them up to the pinnacle of that pyramid called Delighted, which means to delight the customers by giving them something they want or need before they know they want or need it."

Then I give them some examples. Maybe the customer is sick. I'll provide specific examples for someone from the spa, someone from engineering, and someone from the front desk. "So, the customer is in your area and you realize he or she is sick. Think for a moment. Have you ever been sick before?"

I ask an employee to respond. His name tag says Johnny, and he says, "Yes."

I'll say, "Johnny, what do you need when you're sick?"

He'll say, "Well, I'll have some chicken soup."

So I say, "Then you should give it to the customer. You don't have to ask me or ask your manager if you can give chicken noodle soup to a customer in need. You just do it!"

Then I say, "What else do you likely need when you're sick?"

"I need tissues because I'm sneezing a lot."

"Then give the customer some tissues!"

Once you say that, the light bulbs start going off. I still get chills talking about it because it's such a simple concept. It's the art of anticipation that makes a good hotelier.

So, before I get to the Delighted category, I will ask, "Okay, let's relate this to something you're familiar with. How many people in the room go to Starbucks?"

"Oh, I do!"

"I do!"

"I do!"

I'll say, "What do you expect when you go to Starbucks?" and I start at the bottom of the pyramid.

"They'll give us fast service."

"Clean!"

I'll say, "Right."

"Internet."

"Good. Okay, if you went into Starbucks and got just that and left, is it a real WOW? No! What did you request?"

I always make a joke at this point and say, "Are you one of the ones who get that mocha-choco-latte-ya-ya-half-twist-caff on the side?"

Of course, everyone laughs.

Then I say, "So, you expect a hot cup of coffee. That's what you requested, and what did you get? A hot cup of coffee. Did they use your name? You know they ask you your name, and they write it on the cup. What drives me crazy, if they ask you your name, and they take the time to write *Deb* on the cup, and then they say, 'tall latte.' That's a big disappointment, right?"

It's very important in the hospitality industry. You must use your customer's name at least three times in every conversation.

So, back to Starbucks. "And then you get your coffee, and you walk away. However, that's not a WOW experience."

I go back to the hotel side, and I say, "The tissues and the sickness and ..."

Then I ask, "What else could you do? What happens if a guy is carrying a bunch of bags, getting them out of his car? What could you do?"

Then they start engaging in a conversation. "Well, we can ask him if we can take the bags up to his room."

I say, "Exactly. Does the guest need help? Yes. Does he ask for it? No. To *delight* guests, you've got to give them something they want or need before they know they want or need it. That's very important."

Dr. Mark had the opportunity to chat with Garry Ridge, president and CEO of the WD-40 Company, maker of the ever-popular penetrating oil and water-displacing spray, WD-40. The company also produces products like 3-IN-ONE Oil, the heavy-duty hand cleaners Solvol and Lava, and household cleaning products like X-14, Carpet Fresh, Spot Shot, 1001 and 2000 Flushes.

You may never have considered a company like WD-40, whose name stands for "Water Displacement, 40th formula" to have particularly WOW products, but they have been around since 1953. Since that time, the company has grown by leaps and bounds and is now a common household name.

Initially, the WD-40 Company was known as the Rocket Chemical Company. Its small staff of three started in a little San Diego lab to create a line of rust prevention solvents and degreasers for use in the aerospace industry. It took them forty attempts to get a water-displacing formula worked out, hence, the product was named WD-40.

Convair, an aerospace contractor, first used WD-40 to protect the outer skin of the Atlas missile from rust and corrosion. The product so impressed the Convair team that several of their employees snuck some cans of WD-40 out of the plant to use at home. By 1969, the company was renamed for this WOW product. Today the uses for this product number in the thousands. Very few brands will ever match the popularity of WD-40.

A native of Australia, Garry Ridge has been with WD-40 since 1987 in various management positions. He has worked directly with WD-40 in fifty countries. In 2015, the Center for Leadership Innovation and Mentorship Building (CLIMB) named Garry its "Outstanding Business Leader for 2015," citing him as a "walking textbook on effective leadership."

Garry shared his philosophy about creating positive lasting memories and personal magnificence with Dr. Mark:

One of the lovely things we have here at WD-40 is that we don't make mistakes, rather we have "learning moments." Why? Because a "learning moment" is a positive or negative outcome of any situation that can be openly and freely shared, with one objective: to help us become better. To help us, tomorrow, step into a new version of our best self.

We have the opportunity, every day, to step into a new version of our best self. I think that's what's wonderful. Out of that comes the only thing we ever have in life, which is memories. At the end of the day, the only thing we will ever have left is a memory. Everything material will be gone.

We have the opportunity, every day, to step into a new version of our best self.

Our job is to create positive lasting memories. I want you to leave here today with a positive lasting memory. I will leave here today with a positive lasting memory because you've come to visit me. Why? Because I would have learned something from you. You would have given me something I didn't have before. I hope I give you the same. It's the same in business. That's really what it's about.

You know, we're a public company, and we must create positive lasting memories for our shareholders. Interestingly enough, if you look at our track record over the last seventeen years, we've got a pretty enviable growth rate of profit and return. We didn't do that by leaving people on the sidelines. We did it by creating an environment where we allowed people to perform their own personal magnificence daily.

Soundbite FROM DR. MARK

Alexander Hamilton said, "If you don't stand for something, you'll fall for anything." If, however, you do stand for something, then stand up for it and stop people who violate what matters most to you and those for whom you care. Not only will you not fall for anything, you will also have loyal, passionate followers who will help you accomplish anything.

ACTION STEPS

1   Take the opportunity to brainstorm with your team. Ask them what you could do together. What is bigger and bolder and more audacious than anything you have ever done before, yet still in alignment with your corporate or organizational objectives?

2   Now think about how your corporate or organizational objectives might be revised and emboldened if you had a WOW vision.

3   What would a truly WOW vision look like for your organization?

4   If and when you finally achieve that WOW factor, be sure to give the credit and heartfelt appreciation where it is due ... without overshadowing the limelight for others with your own ego.

Not only will you not fall for anything, you will also have loyal, passionate followers who will help you accomplish anything.

FIVE

Mentor in the Moment

*People feel like they belong here, not because
they are welcomed every day, but because we are
doing things every day to help them be better.*

—GARRY RIDGE
President and CEO of the WD-40 Company

WOW factor workplaces are what they are, raved about by
team members as "the best place I ever worked," because
nearly every member in it is somewhat like a Master Gardner.

If you aren't familiar with the term, a Master Gardner has a love
of gardening and a passion for sharing it with others. Despite the
title, they don't typically have a master's degree in the subject.
Rather, they tend to learn something new every day through basic
training classes and hands-on experience, trial, and error. Master
Gardeners get down in the dirt to make things grow. They welcome
the opportunity to help others improve their gardening skills by
passing along the information they have learned. They do it for the
pure joy of it. It's a passion.

WOW factor workplaces don't get to be WOW factor workplaces by accident. They become that way through passionate determination, persistence, unwavering attention to detail, mentoring, and heartfelt leadership.

Sometimes adjustments are required. Adjustments are made all the time in WOW factor workplaces to make things even better than they already are. The adage, "If it ain't broke, don't fix it" is NOT the way WOW factor workplaces become WOW factor workplaces. Sometimes you must break things intentionally to make continuous dramatic improvements that enable WOW to happen.

Refer to my story in Chapter 2 about Bern's Steak House, which was established by Bern Laxer and his wife Gert with little more than the money in their pocket, in Tampa's Hyde Park area back in 1956. (Bern's was initially called the Beer Haven on Howard Avenue.) Ever since Bern passed away at age 78 in 2002, the family has continued to carry on Bern's passion for people and excellence to this very day.

In Bern's honor, son David and daughter-in-law Christina, along with Christopher Sherman, gave the world an insider's look through their beautifully illustrated book, *Bern's: Rare and Well Done*. In this book, they tell how Bern "worked every corner of the kitchen, pitching in on every chore, not only to show he could perform the details of any job but also to observe how well each staff member was working."

In their book, the Laxers shared a story about one of their staff members, Paul DeMeza, lovingly known as "Gil." In Gil's own words, it was "an incredible learning experience to watch Bern, how his mind worked and processed. He was a perfectionist with remarkable attention to detail."

Gil tells a story of how one time, when he oversaw the waiter trainee program, Bern walked by and handed Gil some pieces of mop string he had picked up from an otherwise clean kitchen floor. Gil found thirty-five cents deducted from his next paycheck.

Gil got the message, yet he persevered. When he graduated from being a kitchen trainee to work with the dining room captains, Bern told him, "You're the worst kitchen manager I've ever had. You're too damn nice. But you're going to make one hell of a waiter."

Sometimes you must make adjustments to make WOW happen.

> **Whenever I go on a ride, I'm always thinking of what's wrong with the thing and how it can be improved.**
> —Walt Disney, American Entrepreneur, Animator and Film Producer

Hiring and firing right are both important. One of the best pieces of advice I ever received as a manager—a lesson I wished I had learned much earlier in my career—was "always be interviewing." I thought it strange when I first heard it, but once I understood, I've shared that philosophy with every member of my staff ever since.

The original comment was because in many businesses, headcount must be budgeted and authorized. Of course, even headcount which is budgeted and authorized can be taken away at any time, based on the financial needs of the business. When you have the approval to fill a vacant slot, as a hiring manager, you better be ready to fill that slot (or any slot which might magically become available) with the best possible candidate, as quickly as possible, because that headcount might not remain available very long. The authorization could be taken away at any instant, and you could miss the opportunity to make your best-ever hire.

I also learned along the way (and I also shared *this* with all my staff members), everyone should interview elsewhere from time to time. This is one way to ensure neither the employee nor the business gets complacent. It's crucial for employees to know their value to the outside world.

Likewise, organizations should be made aware if they are not keeping up with competitive marketplace opportunities. You certainly don't want to wait until your best team members have accepted another position elsewhere to finally offer them a raise or a promotion. By then, their hearts and minds are out the door.

> Be on the lookout for chances to move the business ahead by making timely and justifiable staffing adjustments.

As a leader, if you have a good relationship with your staff, you can regularly have open dialogues about expectations. Always be on the lookout for chances to move the business ahead by making timely and justifiable staffing adjustments. When employees are aware of their real market value—or lack thereof—they aren't as likely to be victims, or even in the crosshairs, when layoffs take place. Through external informational interviews, employees are better able to gain valuable industry knowledge and bring new ideas back to the organization. In case an entire organization is shut down, as can happen in cyclical downturns, team members will have a survival strategy at the ready.

Thanks to this insightful and truly invaluable "always be interviewing" advice from one of my best-ever bosses, Todd, I came to love interviewing people. I do this almost everywhere I go, even when I'm out with my family and friends. It's not necessarily about finding a job or a better opportunity for myself; it's usually just about meeting amazing people, learning interesting insights from them, and helping *them* whenever I can. I tend to take particular note of people who are outstanding in their roles and who demonstrate particularly great attitudes and customer service aptitude.

I can't begin to count the number of people I have helped place in *dream jobs,* which had nothing to do with my organization. It's only because I find almost everyone amazing when I ask the right questions, and because I love to do favors for people, to pay it forward. Often, if I introduce them to some other amazing person, real synergy can unexpectedly happen. I do this all the time. And you know what? It makes the world a better place.

Here's one example:

One weekend morning, my husband and I were enjoying an excellent breakfast at one of our local neighborhood cafes. Our server that morning, Debbie, was someone I had not seen before, yet she was a WOW service provider.

I asked Debbie how long she had been in this job. She seemed somewhat embarrassed, and sheepishly said, "Three weeks."

She went on to ask if there was something she had done wrong and if there was anything she could do to improve our experience. I replied, "To the contrary. You are outstanding in this role. You must have worked somewhere stellar before that provided you with some pretty great training."

Debbie blushed and said, "No. This is my first job in years. I have six children, and I stayed home to raise them. I home-schooled all of them. Now my oldest ones are finally getting ready to go out on their own, so I decided to help bring some money into the family. The only food service or customer service experience I have had is from home, cooking for two adults and six children. I have always tried to be a role model to make sure the kids learned their table manners. We eat dinner together every night, and I serve their dinner. That's all the service experience I have ever had. However, I am trying!"

Debbie gave us such a WOW experience, even though she only had a few weeks of experience at the cafe, I could tell she would make a great dining room manager. I wanted to help accelerate her advancement into a position worthy of her skills and abilities. The idea popped into my head that she would be the kind of dining room manager our local country club could use, so I arranged an interview for her there.

While the country club didn't have a dining room manager position immediately available, they hired her to work as a server in the golf course clubhouse restaurant. She was stellar in that job, and the golf club members raved about her.

When a dining room manager's position finally opened in the club's fine dining facility, Debbie was promoted to that position, and they backfilled her server position in the golf course clubhouse restaurant with her oldest son. Not surprisingly, the son's customer service skills were every bit as good as his mother's. It was a win-win for everyone.

Colleen Barrett, Southwest Airlines' President Emeritus and Corporate Secretary, shared this about the importance of mentoring others and paying it forward:

> All the lessons I have had from unbelievable mentors, and I have had many—male and female—I have tried to pay forward to others.
>
> Many times, it's not money, but sometimes it is money. Often when people have said to me, "You've saved my life. What can I do?" I've replied, "Look, you don't owe me anything. I want you, when and if the time comes, if you can do something similar for somebody else, do it. Then send me a note and tell me you've paid me back."
>
> That's all I want because if I hadn't had people do that for me, I wouldn't be sitting here today. And I mean that from the depths of my soul.

Donald Stamets of Auberge Resorts told me this story of how he got started in the hospitality industry:

> Are you ready for this? I was a busboy at Howard Johnson's on the New Jersey Turnpike, exit 1, when I was sixteen years old. After a while, I graduated to server. Then I went to college and transferred from Howard Johnson's in New Jersey to the Howard Johnson's in Seekonk, Massachusetts. It was close to Providence because I went to Johnson & Wales University. I always knew I was a hotel/restaurant guy. I was born to serve.

I think it was because my mom was so sick. I didn't know it when I was young, but I always had to care for her. It made me feel good to make her feel better. You know, I don't think I've ever said that publicly before. Wow. That has to be where it's from.

My brother worked there so, of course, I had to work there. I was the younger brother by two years. He got the job first. I was like, "Hmm. I could do that. I'm better at talking to people than he is."

So I got the job. We worked together for one summer before he went off to college.

I asked Donald, "Did you have a mentor there?"

My gosh. You're taking me back.

No. The managers there, if anything, taught me what not to do. I was a learner at a very young age. They were awful to their employees, screaming and miserable and always in their offices, pointing fingers and telling us what to do.

Because we came from nothing (we grew up on food stamps and welfare), I saw the nicer I was to people, the bigger tip I would get. I think I learned at a very young age if you were friendly and engaged and treated people with respect, they, in turn, would treat you that way.

I interjected, "So it wasn't your manager at Howard Johnson's telling you to treat people with respect?"

No. I was self-taught. Maybe I was motivated because of the money portion. I knew, at home, I didn't have anything. It was nice to have spending money so I could go out with my friends, or go to the movies, or put gas in my car without asking my mom for a dollar or two.

I followed up with, "Did you ever feel like you were swimming upstream there, given the management philosophy?"

No, because they were so NOT involved. We, the monkeys, really ran the zoo there. The waiters ran everything. We were all such a tight-knit family of waiters (or servers, if you will). We just worked together like clockwork. I think in addition to my affiliation with my high school marching band, which had a big influence on my life, working there taught me teamwork, a work ethic, dedication, and respect.

I worked at the Westin Bonaventure in LA right after graduating college. It was a fifteen hundred room hotel with 100,000 square feet of meeting space ... a concrete jungle ... a monster. During the six years I was there, I had eleven promotions.

I was the Food & Beverage Management candidate. I quickly became Assistant Manager of Room Service. Then I was promoted to Dining Room Manager for the Sidewalk Cafe, which is their three-meal-a-day restaurant. Later, I became the Director for the Fine Dining restaurant. Then I became the Director of Restaurants. Eventually, I thought, "I've handled Food & Beverage. I want to try something else."

Every customer must experience an interaction, not a transaction.

So, I jumped over and tried running the front desk. Because of my leadership abilities, even though I didn't know the front desk, they said, "We'll make you a front desk manager." I had learned in college, of course, but I had never really worked the front desk, checking people in and checking people out. But now I'm one of the Managers of the Day of this 1,500 room hotel, working the 7-to-3 shift, the 3-to-11 shift, and the 11-to-7 shift (graveyard), carrying the radios, directing everyone on what to do.

Eventually, I got tired of managing the front desk and said, "I want to try Sales." I was in Sales for a year and a half.

I asked Donald to fast-forward and talk about his hiring philosophies.

An important quote I say to all my leaders is, "Every customer must experience an interaction, not a transaction."

There's a big difference there between a transaction and an interaction. I want to make sure that I engage and interact with my leaders. I trust them to do the job that they need to do versus micromanage them. At the end of the day, does anyone want to be micromanaged? No, they don't.

You hire someone with the smarts and the capacity to do the job for which they were hired. In my leadership style, I like to trust all my associates. I do have to verify they're doing what's right because they may try to pull the wool over my eyes. We could lose a big account or whatever. I give them enough rope to do what they need to do but reel it in a little bit and verify. I really want them to know that I trust them.

I asked him then, "How does that verification piece work? Does it come down to performance reviews?"

I think it's as frequent and as honest as possible. I have found if you wait until the performance review to tell them they did something wrong six or eight months ago, a) it doesn't make them feel good, and b) it's a bad reflection on me.

I think feedback is a gift.

So, it's about feedback and making sure you give that feedback right away, instantaneously. Say, "Look, Deb, you do this really, really well. I loved A, B, and C. But D, E, and F could have been done this way. If you had tweaked it that way, we could have saved money, and we could have made the customer happier," whatever the situation is.

I think feedback is a gift. Whether that is constructive feedback or positive feedback, it has to be viewed as a gift. When customers are telling me we made a mistake, that's one of the first things out of my mouth: "I appreciate you telling me we made a mistake because I do view it as a gift. If I don't know about it, I cannot fix it. So, allow me the opportunity to now go on a diagnostic journey and search upstream to find the root cause, so this doesn't happen to you or anybody else in the future."

So, trust but verify.

I asked next, "Is there a difference in how you go about verifying with different people?"

Wow, great question. Yes. Again, it's an individualized approach. Most people don't want to have anything negative handled in public.

Another thing I always like to say to people is, "Make sure, for all your leaders, you support publicly, and you defend privately."

Going back to the verification process, I have one-on-ones with all my leaders weekly or biweekly, based on their tenure in their position and how comfortable we both are in what they're doing. We always talk about what's on their agenda for the upcoming week.

How can I help them? If they do something, at the time when they are presenting to me, we can review and then I verify at that potential moment. So, it's within days of a project being done. Never wait. However, I always use an individualized approach, one-on-one, in my office.

Another best-ever boss referred to us was Howard Behar, the now-retired president of Starbucks Coffee and author of the book, *It's Not About the Coffee: Lessons on Putting People First from a Life at Starbucks.* During his tenure at Starbucks, Howard helped grow the company from 28 stores to over 15,000 stores spanning five continents.

Howard is well-known for his sense of customers as people, his concern for their needs and his experience of being a part of people's dreams for their lives. In 2018, Howard Behar was honored with a Lifetime Achievement Award at the Pacific Northwest's Executive Excellence Awards, a program which recognizes select Washington state senior executives who have demonstrated extraordinary, consistent leadership in guiding their companies to success.

Dr. Mark queried Howard about performance reviews, stating, "Most people want to avoid performance reviews. What would be your approach?"

Howard responded this way:

> Well, I think it's simple. A performance review ought to be a compilation; whether you make them annual or semiannual, you make your choice. They are just a compilation of all the conversations you had before. The conversations need to be daily.
>
> **I think annual performance reviews—how typical organizations do them—are worthless.**
>
> When you want to work with people on helping them to be better at whatever they're doing, it's in the moment. The best learning happens within the moment. There's nothing better when you see somebody doing something right than to tell him or her in the moment. Why would you wait until the end of the year or the end of the week? You do it now.
>
> The more we're in the moment of doing these things, we're having an ongoing dialogue. Then, when you sit down and you review the year, or you review the past six months, it's just talking about those things which came up before, not hammering them again. It's looking back at your life, taking that movie and rewinding it.

Rather than you doing it, it's the person you're coaching, or you're giving the performance review to who's doing it. You're asking the employee, "Give me your last six months. How have you done?" They'll rehash the things you've talked with them about, the things they've talked about with you.

I think annual performance reviews—how typical organizations do them—are worthless. They have this whole deal; they call it "the sandwich." Give 'em something good, give 'em something bad, and end it with something good. Everybody knows that. That is a trick of the trade.

What makes good relationships? What makes good marriages? Constant communication (the good, the bad, and the ugly). Constant communication ... because you gain trust with each other. Trust is the glue that makes the world go around. Without it, nothing can happen. The way to gain trust is always being there, not just being there at performance review time.

I met Todd Wilcox, chairman of Patriot Defense Group, when he ran for the United States Senate in Florida in 2016. Todd was a decorated combat veteran who, earlier in his career, was commissioned as an infantry officer in the US Army. He went on to serve as a rifle platoon leader with the 101st Airborne Division during Operation Desert Storm. Upon promotion to captain, Todd volunteered for a transfer to the US Army Special Forces

> **If you want the right employee, you've got to mentor them. You've got to develop them over time.**

branch. After earning his Green Beret, he commanded a Special Forces A-team in a counterterrorism role in East Asia.

After eight years of military service, Todd resigned to accept a position with the CIA to join America's global war on terrorism. While completing two years of Arabic studies and then serving from various US embassy postings in the Middle East and North Africa, Todd was also raising two daughters on his own as a single parent. His last assignment with the CIA was on the Joint Terrorism Task Force in the FBI field office in Orlando.

In 2006, Todd founded Patriot Defense Group, a defense contracting company dedicated to serving those who defend America. It was no surprise to learn Todd was recognized in 2015 as an Ernst and Young Entrepreneur of the Year finalist.

Todd had this to say about mentoring the team:

> If you want the right employee, you've got to mentor him or her. You've got to develop employees over time.
>
> That's what I've found out. It's difficult to find people who have the same level of passion when they may or may not be rewarded with the same kind of benefits an owner gets. The harder I work as an entrepreneur, as an owner of a company, if I see that's directly related to profitability, well, the harder I work, the more money I make. It's not necessarily the case for someone who's making twenty or thirty or forty bucks an hour and punching in eight hours a day.
>
> I think that's the critical part where heartfelt leadership comes into play, where you inspire that passion if you can.

In response, I asked Todd, "What do you say to those CEOs who claim, "It's not my job to inspire them. It's up to them to get excited about the job."

Todd replied:

> I'd say they've failed, or they will fail if they don't change their mindset. Leadership is ALL about inspiration. You must inspire people to get things done. Part of that is a paycheck. It's a

reward and punishment system. Some of it's inspirational. Some of it is through admiration. Some of it is out of fear of losing their job or being fired. But whatever the right mix is, you better figure it out quick, especially if you are the CEO.

I asked Todd to share his philosophy on how to create a "Best Place to Work" culture. He shared this:

> When I started this company, I was coming out of a very bureaucratic CIA. I knew I did not want to burden the people who were trying to get the mission accomplished with a lot of bureaucracy. The CIA, like many government agencies, has a lot of processes, a lot of institutional systems and procedures and rules and regulations. So, I wanted to be a little less burdensome when it came to operating.
>
> It also influenced that mantra we have: "No assholes. No idiots." We came from an organization that had a lot of assholes and a lot of idiots. We knew, coming to work on a high operational tempo, doing some very interesting things for national security —sometimes dangerous things—you want to be comfortable. You want to go to work every day enjoying the company of the people to your left and right. So, we tried to foster that kind of culture as we built the company.
>
> But I also saw three or four steps ahead. I knew I wanted to build an organization of people with a culture conducive to getting the job done and serving our clients. We built those very necessary processes and systems in place, knowing we'd get there eventually, even though it was just me and one or two guys, or me and three or four folks. Now we've got more than two hundred employees across all three businesses. So, we developed those systems, those management systems we knew were critical, but we stayed away from the ones I thought were burdensome in the organization I came from.
>
> In the CIA, you have periodic performance appraisals. Here, we don't have those. You know daily whether you are doing a good

No assholes. No idiots.

job or not. The fact you're getting a paycheck means you are probably doing a pretty good job. There's always counseling and critique and criticism that comes along. But what should be done every single day, as a manager, is mentoring a subordinate.

We don't have these "fill in the blank" or "circle the bubble" forms or try to figure out whether someone is meeting performance requirements or not. If you're still here the next day, you're probably doing what you're supposed to be doing. That's an example of what we decided NOT to do with some long, drawn-out performance appraisal which gets filled out once a quarter, or twice a year, and goes into a file and never gets looked at again.

> **If you're not talking to people every single day, then I would argue you're not effectively communicating, managing, mentoring, and developing them.**

I asked him, "Do you have a formal performance appraisal system, or is it an everyday thing?"

Todd responded:

It's every single day.

Nobody is in charge of more than five people. You can't effectively lead, mentor, and develop more than four or five direct reports. Nobody has more than four or five direct reports in this company.

I followed with, "How did you learn that?"

By experience. Part of it comes from the doctrine of the military.

In the military, if you look at the line-block diagram of any organization, there are usually four or five direct subordinates working for any one commander. A battalion commander has three or four company commanders, maybe a couple of specialty folks, an executive officer (XO) who runs the staff, and the staff is five or six people.

Likewise, on the other side of that, I saw at the CIA where one manager would have twenty people working for him, and it was completely dysfunctional.

It was a result of seeing examples, both good and bad, both sides of that coin of what works and what doesn't work. I just created this to reflect what I thought worked along the way.

Curious, I responded with another question, "Why doesn't it work when you have fifteen to twenty direct reports? Why is just four or five better?"

Todd offered this:

Part of it is time. There are limited resources. You don't have enough time to talk to more than four or five or six people in a single day. If you're not talking to people every single day, then I would argue you're not effectively communicating, managing, mentoring, and developing them. Part of it's just a time factor.

I think it may also depend on the functionality of the organization. What is the organization's intent? What is its purpose? What is its mission?

Has it just become a pencil drill?

If it's a factory line and you've got one factory manager and people who are doing what they're doing, doing the same thing every single day; i.e., "I bolt these tires onto the car. That's all I do." Once you get that down, you probably don't need much mentoring after that. Maybe in that kind of an organization fifteen to twenty people is feasible.

This organization is meeting the demands of some of the most elite warriors in our Special Operations and Intelligence community (one of our companies does very sophisticated and complicated logistical tasks overseas, in hostile environments). Then we have a private investigative firm that digs into some unique challenges for our clients, in terms of risk management and risk mitigation. Those are nebulous kinds of operating environments. I think that requires a different type of leadership and a different kind of force structure. I believe it is more in line with the military.

I then asked him, "What would you advise those companies that have a formal annual or semi-annual appraisal process?"

If it works for them, great. But how much time does it take? Do a little analysis to see how many man-hours are put into it by the people being mentored and counseled, by the people doing the counseling, by HR who must file these things. What's being done as a result of it? Has it just become a pencil drill?

That's what it became in the military. Promotions were based on appraisals, so you dare not develop a competent leader who may have a few areas in which he needs to improve. If you were too candid in those appraisals, he wouldn't get promoted. In the military, at the time, you were out. It's up or out.

What happened was, it got so diluted and so watered down it was meaningless. Everybody got the top block. There would be some narrative in there, and you might be able to discern and read between the lines when it would come to a promotion board, but you were being dishonest or doing a disservice to those individuals by not being more critical. Like I said, it just became a pencil drill.

I would ask those executives and leaders to really analyze it. What's your payout? What's the result of this system, this process? How much is going into it, and what do you get out of it?

Garry Ridge, CEO of WD-40, had this to say about "figuring it out":

When I started executing more and more of these principles: *Care, Candor, Accountability, Responsibility, Learning, Teaching, Respect, and Fun,* I doubted a little bit, in the beginning, whether it would deliver the results. But I had it in my gut. Throughout my life growing up so far, I have thought, "If you could stick this out, it could work."

I am now totally convinced, and the record is written. I think my gift can be saying, "Hey, you've got to stick with it."

If you get these few basic principles of *Care, Candor, Accountability, Responsibility, Learning, Teaching, Respect and Fun* right, then, if you stick with it, you will be successful. You're going to have ups and downs. So, it's just that confidence.

I remember when I went back to the University of San Diego (USD). I did my master's degree in leadership there. I'd just been appointed CEO of WD-40. Someone said to me, "You've just been appointed CEO of WD-40, and you're going back to university to get a master's degree in leadership? Aren't you already a leader?"

I said, "No. I want to go and confirm what I think I know and learn what I don't know."

> **If you get these few basic principles of *Care, Candor, Accountability, Responsibility, Learning, Teaching, Respect and Fun* right, then, if you stick with it, you will be successful.**

As I went through that program at USD, there would be examples which would come up, and I would think, "I thought that was right," but there was no academic proof I could put toward it. Now I have enough proof, and I just turned up the volume on it.

I went through the program and at the end, I think I confirmed a lot more than I learned, but that was well worth the journey because I got that confirmation. What I'm saying is, I've gotten more confident in the execution.

When things started to maybe not go in the right direction, I said, "I've got to stick with it."

This *Care, Candor, Accountability, Responsibility, Learning Teaching, Respect, and Fun* are things I think are essential. I'm going to stick with it. It's paid off.

I can say it. It's consistency, persistence, never give up.

At the bottom of my emails, it says: *Believe in yourself. Never give up. Take one day at a time. We all have something significant yet to do.*

During their interview, Dr. Mark said this to Garry, "It's easy to tell walking into this place you are not only trusted and admired, you are also loved. Are you aware of how loved you are?"

I think—I hope my care for them is respected by them, which then translates into them having a form of love for me. I think you have to earn that.

I think *Belonging* is the biggest driver. Belonging has to have proof. People feel like they belong here, not because they are welcomed every day, but because we are doing things every day to help them be better. We help educate them. We are helping them feed their families. We help them deal with their stresses of life.

Just last Friday we had a Lunch-and-Learn. We had someone in here, giving people a two-hour session on Stress Management. We got a couple of chairs in here and had massage therapists in here during that time. That sort of stuff costs little. Why do we do it? We want people to be feeling good about themselves, in many ways, not just emotionally but physically.

I think what's great is in our last Employee Opinion Survey— with a 99% positive response globally—the number one measure was: "At WD-40 Company I'm treated with respect and dignity."

The number two was: "I know what results are expected of me, and I'm free to share a differing point of view." These were all within a basis point of 99%, the top five or six of them. Okay, we get it.

It's kind of humbling to think I'm loved. I didn't do it to be loved.

Soundbite FROM DR. MARK

One of the greatest tragedies in life is getting to the end of your life and looking back, and realizing it was mediocre...and didn't have to be that way.

Focus on a future nobody has screwed up yet. Ask others, "Going forward, how can I (or this thing) be better?"

Then listen to whatever they have to say.

Don't criticize yourself but think of what you can improve on.

Avoid the counterproductivity of excuses, blame, not meeting commitments, or keeping promises. Counter concerns of inadequacy by directly addressing deficiencies.

What separates the people who habitually achieve their goals and create the results they desire from those who don't? You already know the answer. It's follow-through.

ACTION STEPS

1 Think about the situations you have within your current workplace. If you could wave a magic wand to make things better than they are today, what kind of changes would you make?

2 Of the modifications you might recommend, which actions are within your span of control? If any, what can you do to activate improvements, starting tomorrow?

3 Of those changes that are not within your span of control, who might have the authority to make such changes? Have you spoken to them about your ideas, including what is in it for them to consider making such changes?

4 If the person with authority waved his or her magic wand and put you in charge as King or Queen for a day (or a month, or a year), what resources would you need to activate these improvements and just what steps would you take to make it all happen, starting tomorrow?

SIX

High Expectations

The worst disservice you can do is NOT tell somebody when he or she is not making the grade.

—COLLEEN BARRETT
President Emeritus, Southwest Airlines

To build and maintain a WOW factor workplace, it's crucial to pay attention when individual performance is not up to par. Your best performers can become demotivated when those around them are allowed to slack off or—worse yet—when underperformers are promoted merely to get them out of the department. Nothing will demoralize an otherwise highly motivated team faster than promoting an underperformer.

Back in the good old days, before American society became so litigious, every IBM sales branch office was held firmly and strictly accountable for maintaining high employee satisfaction and high customer satisfaction. These two business drivers were measured annually through surveys which were conducted worldwide and measured down to the sales branch office level. Back then, the target goal for employee satisfaction was a score of 95%. The target goal for customer satisfaction was 98%.

One year when the annual employee satisfaction survey numbers were reported, one sales office achieved an Employee Satisfaction score somewhere well below the target. Surprisingly, nothing seemed to happen, at least not anything discernable to the office staff at the time.

Two weeks later, when the annual Customer Satisfaction survey numbers were reported on a Friday afternoon, this same sales branch office learned their Customer Satisfaction score had also come in well below the target.

The following Monday morning when the staff of the low-scoring sales branch office arrived for work, they found all the managers' offices empty. The branch office manager, the two sales managers, and the system engineering manager had all been fired. Their offices had been cleaned out over the weekend. IBM's target standards were to be achieved, and such low performance was not tolerated. Period. No excuses. End of story.

Due to US labor laws, such drastic repercussions don't generally seem to happen these days. I can't begin to count the number of managers—at all levels and from virtually every industry segment and within the government—say how *impossible* it is to fire an underperforming employee. "HR won't let me," or "It's just too hard because of the legal ramifications" are just a few of the usual excuses.

On the other hand, WOW factor workplaces typically have a well-documented set of behavioral standards and performance expectations. Great leaders, heartfelt leaders, all lead by example. They believe in their people, and they accept total responsibility for the team's and each team member's results. Blaming others is not an option. The buck stops with the leader.

When people aren't meeting agreed-to expectations, heartfelt leaders, leaders of WOW factor workplaces, will collaborate with the underperformer to jointly develop an improvement plan which spells out SMART goals (i.e., Specific, Measurable, Achievable, Reasonable, and Time-bound). Each improvement objective is agreed to by both sides. Each party is responsible for holding the other accountable to his or her end of the agreed-to bargain.

> **High expectations are the key to everything.**
> —Sam Walton, Founder of Walmart and Sam's Club

If the manager fails to uphold his or her end of the deal, you start again. If the underperformer fails to achieve each of the SMART goals agreed to in the mutually developed Performance Improvement Plan (PIP), the exit plan agreed to in the Consequences section of the Improvement Plan is implemented. It's that simple. It may be time-consuming for the manager, but it wastes a whole lot less time and causes far less suffering for everyone in the impacted organization over the long run.

I haven't had to put too many underperformers on such a plan, but I never hesitated to do so when it was necessary. With a chronically unhappy or incapable employee, or an obvious cultural misfit, doing so was always the right thing to do, and in the end, ALL the team members thanked me, even the underperformer. The underperformer either got his or her act together, or moved on to something more in line with his or her passions and desires, which was often the underlying issue in the first place.

As a result, over the years my teams virtually always exceeded our objectives, and we had superior camaraderie. We never lacked for great candidates to fill openings because the best people wanted to work in our WOW organization, and we kept a steady stream of pre-interviewed potential superstars waiting in the wings. It is impressive how high performance begets more high performers.

Now let's hear from some of our other WOW factor workplace leaders to see what they had to say.

According to Colleen Barrett of Southwest Airlines:

> I have had to look dear friends in the eye and tell them they couldn't keep a job because of something they'd done or whatever. Or I couldn't recommend them for another job because of whatever, and I still retained the friendship. You know, that's hard. But if you're just honest with people, I think the worst disservice you can do is NOT tell somebody when they are not making the grade. That's just ridiculous.

I asked Teresa Laraba, a longtime business associate of Colleen's at Southwest, "What do you think when a leader says, 'It's not my job to get people to want to work here. It's not my job to motivate them. They're either motivated, or they're not.'"

Teresa responded with this:

> That's a very interesting comment; it's one we talk about a lot here. There does have to be a core sense in individuals that motivates them to come to work. They must want to get up in the morning and want to live their life.
>
> But once they get to your place of employment, especially as a leader, it is your responsibility to make sure the workplace is as engaging and welcoming as it can be. Especially in our

case, you are living out what people expect at Southwest Airlines: a caring environment.

There are employees whom I've met over the years who were not unmotivated to be here; they were just not happy individuals. And no, it's not my responsibility to make those people who are unhappy in their lives happy. But it is my responsibility when people come to work, and they've done their part, to make sure I'm doing my part. I'm ensuring the environment's engaging, and I'm showing my Servant's Heart in my leadership to them because they spend a lot of time at work. Sometimes they spend more time at work than at home.

I've had people thank me for telling them they didn't need to work here because they've opened their lives to something completely different— this wasn't the right place for them.

As leaders, you are responsible for keeping employees engaged, in helping keep morale up, and tapping into why an employee may not be happy. Maybe they don't appear to be motivated, but they have been motivated until now. You can't just ignore that. You must find out what's going on. There is obviously something that's happened. You need to reach out to them.

We do not subscribe to "you leave your problems at the door." You do, in the sense the customer shouldn't have to pay for your employees' problems, but as leaders you ought to know what's going on with them and find out if there's something that's stopping your employees from delivering on their work promise that day.

If you take the time to get to know your employees as you work with them every day, as you walk by them every day, if you have just two or three one-minute engagements as you walk through your workplace, it builds. If you don't bother asking employees how they're really doing except for every six months, or if you don't stop to talk to them except once a year when you give them their performance appraisal, it is going to take too much time, because you're trying to build a relationship in a ten-minute conversation when you should have been building a relationship every day.

Every time you interact with employees, you should be building those relationships. They will be so much more loyal to the company and to your mission if they know you care as a leader. If you don't invest that time, or you have fooled yourself into thinking you don't have time, or you don't look at every opportunity to interact as time invested in an employee, it's your loss, their loss, and the company's loss.

I know by the response I get from people, even people who no longer work here, whom I've terminated, who still correspond with me. I've had people thank me for telling them they didn't need to work here because they've opened their lives to something completely different. This wasn't the right place for them. Then you know you've made a difference in somebody's life, not just a difference in his or her eight-to-five life.

During his interview with Howard Behar of Starbucks Coffee, Dr. Mark reflected, "There is a difference between feeling liked by someone and being evaluated by someone based on how well you are functioning. That can feel dehumanizing. Can you talk about that?"

Here was Howard's reply:

I think everything starts with that relationship piece. There's this old saying, probably you know it: "People don't care how much you know. They want to know how much you care." That is so true. I don't care how much you know as a leader or as a boss. Even if you're technically proficient in a technical organization, they want to work with people they like and with people they believe like them.

Look, you can like somebody, you can love somebody, but they may not be able to perform in the position they currently have. It doesn't make them bad people. We have this good/ bad thing based on performance.

Let's assume all people are good. Let's make that assumption: all people are good. As long as you keep that always at the forefront, the person I'm talking to who isn't performing is still a good person, who still has lots of redeeming qualities, then, his or her performance is a different thing. It may be something the person can do, is not able to do, maybe could do in a different kind of job, or maybe do in another company, whatever it happens to be. Everybody has a place.

However, you can still love them; you can still care about them. When they know that, they will do everything they can not to let you down, not to let their teammates down, and not to let themselves down. Sometimes, though, no matter what they do, they can't make the grade.

You see that all the time. I don't care what the job is. It's probably more nebulous in administrative positions. Of course, in sales jobs or marketing jobs, it's probably more specific. Performance standards are clear about what needs to be done. But just because an employee didn't make the number doesn't mean he or she is a bad person.

When you set that kind of thing in motion, then the discussion is different. You don't have to say, "You're not performing." The employee will tell you he or she is not performing. You don't have to say anything. You ask the question, "How are you doing? How do you feel you are doing in your job?"

Britt Berrett, former President of Texas Health Presbyterian Hospital-Dallas, shared this:

It's not to say you condone bad behavior. You don't. You love the organization and the purpose and the meaning and the reason for its existence so much you're willing to have the crucial conversation. You're willing to say, "Listen, for us to fulfill the mission of this organization, this is what we need to accomplish. Are you up for it? Is this where you want to be? If it's not, let us know."

Time after time, I found that to be very successful. When you have that conversation with someone who perhaps is not in the right place at the right time, the team around rejoices ... and it grows.

Right now, we've got three thousand employees. We've cut about ten percent of the workforce. The intent wasn't, "Hey, listen. Let's cut." The intent was, "It's getting more challenging with healthcare reform. We have got to do more to be more efficient." We cut ten percent of the workforce, and our employee engagement went through the roof. It was because, concurrent with those very purposeful business decisions, we did so with a tremendous amount of heart.

Sure, some folks didn't like it. Those who were the whiners and the losers and the jerks, they had grown into that for a reason. I think there was a sense of relief when they were released.

If there is someone on that team, regardless of who it might be, who doesn't bless the lives of the rest, if he or she is not in a place to help and support us, that someone has gotta go.

I recall when I got a new job. I was on the Executive Team. I went in and interviewed every member of the Executive Team. In conversations with them about how things were going, how they were doing, and how they worked with the other members of the team, one individual said, "I can work with the CFO. I don't really trust the CFO, but I can work with the CFO."

> **Create an environment where there's respect, and there's cohesion, and there's trust. All those things are the key to a very dynamic and successful organization.**

I said, "Help me understand what that means: 'I don't trust her.'"

This person said, "I don't think the CFO's intents are for the betterment of care here."

I said, "Well, that's an interesting perspective. You used the word 'trust.' It's a very powerful word."

He said, "No, I truly don't trust her. I think when a decision has to be made, she will do it for financial benefit, not for the betterment of the patient."

Further, he said, "That's what my role is: to protect the organization from the CFO."

It was a huge red flag for me. So, as I went through the rest of the interviews, I started probing at the roles each individual played. I found this individual—not the CFO, but the other—didn't get it.

You've got to trust the team. You've got to respect the roles they play. The CFO comes with a skill set that's unique and adds dialogue that is rich and purposeful and meaningful. Within two weeks, I had to let that other individual go. There's got to be a place of trust.

Then I worked with the CFO, who admittedly may have had some communication challenges. But she was true and faithful to the greater purpose of the organization. My point being that some individuals need to go. To further the mission, you've got to be willing to clean house.

I'm always fearful of an organizational leader who has a favorite, who seems to be their go-to person, to the demise of the dynamics within the team. I think when you work with peak performers, that is a dilemma. How do you keep on encouraging them, but not to the detriment to the rest of the members of the team?

Sometimes I feel like I'm a football coach.

I've got that right now. I've got some unbelievable talent, just great people. I need to create an environment where there's respect, and there's cohesion, and there's trust. All those things are the key to a very dynamic and successful organization.

Sometimes I feel like I'm a football coach. I look at the day-to-day activities, and I know I can't be on the field. I've got to support the team as they execute on strategies. Amid the battle, sometimes you've got to make changes.

That's why I love hockey. Hockey is never-ending. You're sending in shifts. Unlike football, where it's stop-and-go, stop-and-go, stop-and-go, hockey is continual. The puck is moving, and the great hockey players are skating to where the puck will be, not where the puck was. Sometimes you pull the goalie. Sometimes you switch a line. Sometimes the dynamics aren't there. That's okay. You shift, and you move. Yeah, that's a great metaphor for leadership for me.

When I commented to Britt, "I've heard some leaders say they don't have time to get involved in people's lives. What would you say to that?" he replied this way:

I can understand that. I can absolutely understand there is a sense of accomplishment by objectively doing things, regardless of what the impact is, regardless of the emotions, regardless of the influence it has on the team. I think that is short-lived.

A perfect example is FTE control. All these executives are looking at FTE control. We look at what we must cut: Full Time Equivalents, staffing. I guess better restated would be, I think some leaders look at salaries and wages and benefits and look at it very, very objectively. They know how many employees they have, how many they can cut, how many they can add, and what their benefits are.

Regrettably, they're not widgets. We keep on saying they're widgets. They're not widgets. They're people and individuals. While it might take a little bit more time to understand the nature of the individual, the long-term impact is more powerful.

There's the Big Bang Theory, or there's the Effective Utilization Theory. The literature on this is very profound. Transformational leaders get to know the team, understand the team, and invest in the team. The results are superior. *Best Places to Work* organizations have superior results to the others. *Best Places to Work* characteristics demonstrate they care about the team.

In my current organization, we do care about the team. We care enough about the mission and the purpose to make some tough decisions. Does it take more time? Yeah, it does. Do you need to look farther out on the horizon? Absolutely.

The challenge is, are you willing to invest the time and the energy for it?

When you go through tough economic times, I've experienced two theories. There's the Big Bang Theory, or there's the Effective Utilization Theory. The Big Bang Theory tells you to cut out twelve employees. You downsize the department. Effective Utilization means you say to yourself, "Who are the best players on that team? Who do we move off the team to realize the goals we've set for ourselves?"

The Big Bang is very popular because you can objectively say, "Well, I've eliminated this number of employees." Effective Utilization asks, "What are they doing? How are they doing?"

You look at the roles and all the process improvements. You care about the individual. Our experience has indicated Effective Utilization works better than Big Bang. But it is seemingly simpler to cut people.

I then asked, "What do you recommend to those who feel they have been assigned impossible objectives by their boss or the Board of Directors?"

Britt stated:

> If I re-center myself on what my purpose is, then I think I'm a little bit bolder and more innovative.

My response to that would be "Welcome to life." You know, boo hoo hoo.

In some of the presentations we've had, in the same room individuals will say, "Well, I work for the military and that will never work."

Then someone a couple of rows back will say, "I work in the military and that will work extremely well."

Some people will say, "I work for venture capitalists and they'll never accept long-term success. They want it here and now."

Others will say, "I work for venture capitalists, and they unleash the potential of things I didn't think I could do."

I think it's an attitude. I'm reminded we're on a journey. There are a lot of life experiences. You make mistakes. They'll be times when it's seemingly impossible. I have felt that. There's no question; everyone does. If I re-center myself on what my purpose is, then I think I'm a little bit bolder and more innovative.

I think any government structure has high expectations. One thing I look at is velocity and trajectory. What's your pace? How fast are you moving? What's your trajectory? Where is your glide path? To those individuals who use that as an excuse, I would tell them to figure it out.

Todd Wilcox of the Patriot Defense Group commented this way about dealing with the financial realities which can sometimes cause downsizings to occur:

We had the sequester, for example, where we dropped two million dollars off the top line almost overnight because the military cut ten percent from its expenses. That caused us to have to make some adjustments quickly. We had to downsize in Afghanistan. We went from a hundred and thirty people to sixty people within a week because of changes in the environment.

"How did you do that?" I asked.

Todd responded:

You let people go. Basically, you cut off your arm to save the body. We would have bled out, in terms of cash, had we left most people on staff. There's a different category of contract and full-time employees who understand that's the way it happens when a contract goes a different direction. The first thing to cut is overhead and people.

There's been some adjusting along the way. It's not that we implement a strategy and we're so rigid to that plan we can't adjust. We always take that input and relearn and retool as we go.

I replied, "You've successfully grown this business from $0 to $60M in ten years. What's your advice for CEOs who aren't as successful as they'd like to be?"

Todd reflected:

There are so many variables, especially in this business environment we're in now, with all the regulation and the very oppressive tax regime we have in place. I attribute most of my success to luck. I was lucky and in the right place at the right time.

Now, luck favors the prepared and we were ready to seize upon that, but we did a lot of preparation and got ready for the opportunities that came our way, knowing we would come across these opportunities.

If things aren't working, my advice would be to step back and try to analyze why they're not working. Start with yourself. Is it you and your leadership style? Is it your inability to communicate? Is it your inability to set milestones and formulate a plan to get there and implement it?

In response, I asked, "How can you be 100% honest with yourself?"

Todd conjectured:

I think it depends on how old you are. The older you get, as I'm turning fifty this year, the more reluctant you are to change. But I think you must be honest with yourself. I think you must look in the mirror and say, "Is it me, or is it the organization?"

If it's you and the organization, then you've got to be prepared to change both of those. I would step back and do some self-evaluation ... a gut check.

Then look at the organization. Are the right people in the right places? If you are the person who hires the people, you're probably the one who is most reluctant to fire them. I've found that out over the last ten or twelve years.

Again, going back to the *no assholes, no idiots* rule, I thought I was a pretty good judge of character. As time went by, I realized the people we needed to fire, many times, were the people I had hired. It was usually six months after the fact when we fired them. We should have done it sooner.

> **Culture is so important to what we do. We hire slow and we take our time to evaluate people, but we fire fast.**

As I jumped into the campaign to run for the United States Senate, I turned the reins over to my COO. There have been several times when he'd come to me and say, "There's this person we've counseled. We've tried to help him improve, but it's not working."

I'd say, "Well, then, you need to fire him now."

Fast forward three or four months. He comes back to me and says the same thing. I say, "Whoa. I told you, you should have fired him back then."

Ultimately the result is the same. It's usually six months too late when they decided to fire him.

I found that in myself. The people I was most reluctant to get rid of were the people I hired, because how could I be wrong?

It's gotten easier as we've grown. In the beginning, I was looking for the asshole and the idiot. But we've been so successful at developing that culture and infusing that mantra into the culture, everybody else picks it up quickly. It's almost like antibodies. If somebody doesn't fit, we know well within three or four months this is not going to be a good fit.

Culture is so important to what we do. We hire slow, and we take our time to evaluate people, but we fire fast. That was some lesson along the way. Again, because I was hiring most people in the beginning, in the first half of the company's life, I was reluctant to get rid of them. As we've formalized that process of hiring people, I'm not hiring everybody now. It's developed over time.

You don't have to be an asshole to hold people accountable.

Usually, they will display some type of "getting into a groove." So, we try to shake things up, move people around a little bit. We try to develop everybody for the next level of responsibility. You can see when people get comfortable. That's usually the first indication they're going to start slacking off.

There's no room here for mediocrity. When we start to see those indicators, that's when we begin to focus in on the individual. It's usually two levels of management who are focusing in on the issue. It's daily and weekly counseling until we get him back on course. We are very candid about it.

That's kind of the approach we've taken. It's not the Harvard Business School model, but it's working for us.

You have a responsibility to the organization. You have a responsibility to your clients, especially in the business world. You don't have to be an asshole to hold people accountable.

I wouldn't associate heartfelt leadership with being soft. I think it's just more emotionally attached, more empathetic to the people around you, and perhaps a realization you don't know everything. You're not necessarily the smartest guy in the room. If you want the organization to thrive, then you must get the buy-in of everybody involved. That's how I would define it.

Culture is a big part of what I think heartfelt leadership comes down to.

When I asked Todd, "How have you dealt with those situations when people don't buy into your leadership style?" he responded:

While we are very collaborative and it's collegial, we have a very flat chain of command. We don't have much patience for incompetence. If you don't buy into it, then maybe there's another place for you. Maybe this isn't the place for you. We allow people to make mistakes and we allow people to work autonomously within the confines of what it is we're trying to get accomplished. A lot of times, people just don't fit in the culture.

Culture is a big part of what I think heartfelt leadership comes down to. Can you develop a culture within your organization which allows for that kind of style? Do you groom and develop the people who work for you in such a way they're going to respond to that kind of leadership style?

I would say as soon as you think you need to seriously decide whether that person is the right person to be on the bus and if he's in the right position, it's probably already too late. You probably already figured out you should have fired him a long time ago or should have moved him into a different position.

That's been the one lesson that's been recurring, the one I've been hammering my subordinates on: "Look. I've been telling you all along. I've made these mistakes in not firing people fast enough."

If somebody doesn't fit the organization, by the time you
realize it, you should have realized it a long time ago. The
light doesn't just go off one day and, okay, the guy is out. It's
usually a cumulative effect over time. There are some tripwires
along the way.

That's probably the biggest one. If I'd have done that sooner
with some of the people, we might not have lost some of the
value which came along with their catastrophic failures, because
we didn't fire them fast enough.

When I asked Todd about the downsides of waiting too long, he
replied:

Well, if it's an asshole, he's probably alienated a lot of other
people. Some of them might be your customers, so you lose
revenue. It might have been coworkers who didn't want to
sit by this guy every single day, and maybe they go to work
for somebody else. You've just invested all the startup effort
which goes into bringing an employee on and getting him or
her trained up and ready to go. Now you've got turnover when
you didn't need to all because you didn't get rid of the asshole
fast enough.

If it's an idiot and he screwed something up, in our line of work
it could mean somebody gets killed. It could be a failed contract.
Sometimes, if you fail a contract with the government, you can be
barred from future contracts. There are some severe implications
that go along with it. It's reputational exposure. It's legal
exposure. It's financial risk. There are so many implications
with incompetence. It can destroy an organization.

There are some serious downsides to not firing people fast
enough, which can all come to fruition in one form or fashion.

I then asked him, "Once you finally get them out, what are the
impacts on the mood and productivity of the organization?"

Todd claimed:

It validates we should've done it sooner. That's why I've learned that lesson over time.

Like I said, in the early days, it was me looking for the asshole and the idiot. As we developed this culture, it was all of them. If it was somebody I hired and was one of my direct reports, and I didn't let him go, it wasn't until the person was fired when they all came to me and said, "We should have done it sooner."

I'd say, "Well, you should have told me sooner."

Again, there was this natural human instinct. If I hired them and they didn't turn out, that's my failure. So, there was reluctance on my part. That is what has come to fruition over time. You instantly see the difference, and it validates the fact you should have done it sooner. We've been through it three, four or five times now. Afterward, everybody heaves a deep sigh of relief. "Wow. Glad that guy is gone."

Why would we have a bully in the company?

Where was this angst before? Why didn't I know about it? That caused me to get into that reevaluation cycle, to go back and look at myself, at my management style. Why didn't I see in my other employees that this guy was cancerous? We learned and retooled and moved on from there.

Tim Hindes of Stay Metrics brought up one big question he is sometimes asked: How does he deal with people who are bullying in his company?

My answer is, "Why would we have a bully in the company? That's not who we are."

Ask not only, "How do we stop it?" but "How did it even start? We don't treat people that way."

Then when you create a company, when a new person is coming in, remember how it was when you were new. Remember how inept you felt and everything? Well, that's the way that person is going to feel. Your job in life is to make him or her feel warm and comfortable, and NOT judge the person early on.

I think when you can create a welcoming culture, it's going to be good for the company.

When I asked Rein Preik of Chemcraft International how he overcame the "blame syndrome," which can sometimes occur between departments. Rein had this to say:

Let's say we have a situation where the salespeople were saying, "The products out of R&D or manufacturing aren't working. They are no good."

Then R&D or manufacturing says to sales, "The problem is you guys don't know how to sell it" or "You're not instructing the customer how to use it properly."

You can get into situations like this which can be solved easily. You take them both to the customer, and you have a big meeting, a powwow with the customer. With the customer involved, you talk about the promises you have made and how everyone is working hard on this problem.

I dealt with the owners (which is much easier, by the way) or the general manager. Very seldom did we have to deal with committees because the companies we dealt with were not that large. You help the customer become part of the solution, or the customer comes up with the solution.

Sometimes the customer would say, "Oh yeah, we can change our line a little bit. It could work like this."

Then our product people would say, "This is going to save so much money."

So, we would try it. Generally, it would work, and most people were happy. We'd get the people in development happy, and the people in sales were happy, and the customer is happy because he's right in it and he thinks he's part of your company. If you can do that, you have somebody who will be loyal for a long time ... if you make the customer feel like part of your company. It can be done.

We've done it with several large companies. I've been to the owners' houses in the evenings. I would knock on their doors and we would discuss something. We might have disagreements, but if they have confidence in you, you know what? It's kind of fun.

Soundbite FROM DR. MARK

Currently, we can't afford to have people not be held accountable. When you are delegating something to someone, there are two things you want to do after having told someone what to do.

Don't say: "Do you understand what I have asked you?"

Instead, say: "What do you understand about what I have asked you, and why is it important to what we are doing here?"

When you do that, they feel treated as a person instead of as a function.

The second question, to make it stick, is to say: "In the event, for any reason going forward, you are not able to do what you have just promised you will do, how shall I deal with you? All I am concerned about is you get the job done. I know certain things may distract you. I'm not interested in punishing you, so how shall I deal with you?"

What you will discover is you will be much more comfortable with confronting the person if he or she doesn't follow through. These two questions can save you a lot of grief and get you more accountability going forward.

ACTION STEPS

1   How does your organization measure performance at the individual and organizational levels?

2   Are employees and managers held accountable to measurable standards when it comes to customer satisfaction and employee satisfaction?

3   If so, are the standards set high in your estimation or is mediocre performance tolerated?

4   If mediocre performance is the norm in your workplace, can you see a corollary in how your organization ranks in comparison to other organizations within your industry?

5   When established performance targets are not achieved, what kind of corrective action is typically taken, if any?

6   Based on what you know now, what changes would you put in place to ensure accountability at all levels to high-performance standards?

SEVEN

No Excuses

You own this. There's nobody else
who owns this so get over it.
—HOWARD BEHAR
former President, Starbucks Coffee

Some people tend to hold themselves back. They hold themselves back because they think they aren't as good as others or as prepared as others to assume a leadership role. This may be because they haven't had as much education or because they came from a low-income family or any of a whole variety of reasons. Excuses, excuses.

If there is one thing I have learned over the years, nothing holds us back from WOW factor success more than ourselves. If we aren't wildly successful at helping other people become wildly successful, there is only one person to blame. You own it.

I was asked to speak at a STEM conference (Science, Technology, Engineering, and Math) for female PhD students at the University of California at San Diego. Even though I started my college career as a math major at UCLA and I had an MBA (not a PhD), I initially felt a bit intimidated at the thought of speaking to over 100 PhD students on the topic, How to Have Your Cake and Eat It, Too. Then I reminded myself I had been mentoring some of the best and brightest high-potential leaders, including CEOs and other senior executives, for years. I could certainly handle this simple speaking engagement.

As I usually do before I speak, I arrived at the event somewhat early. I introduced myself to several of the attendees to learn more about them and find out just what they were hoping to learn at the conference. I typically do this so I can adjust my talk on the fly to make it as relevant and personal as possible, no matter what size audience I may be addressing.

Before that day, I had been impressed with the increasing number of women across the US who were obtaining graduate and postgraduate degrees. Year after year, women had earned most doctoral degrees. I was glad to know women weren't holding themselves back any longer.

As I spoke with these PhD candidates, I learned that several of them had no idea what they would do with their hard-earned education. A good percentage of them had majored in non-science subjects as undergraduates. Finding their initial career options limited or disappointing after graduating from college, or when they found they weren't getting the kind of respect they felt they deserved from men in the business world, some of these women decided to go back to obtain a graduate degree of some sort, perhaps in psychology or some other area of social science. After receiving a master's degree and their next jobs still didn't live up to their expectations, some of these women figured they might get more respect—and possibly earn higher incomes—if they obtained a doctoral degree.

So here they were.

I was honestly quite taken aback by that. At this point, every ounce of intimidation I had felt before my arrival vanished. These women needed help.

What I learned from this experience was these highly degreed women were no different from the vast majority of "high-potentials" we mentored in the leadership development company I founded following my 30+ years working in Fortune 500 America.

> **Everyone wants a magical solution to their problem, and everyone refuses to believe in magic.**
> The Mad Hatter from
> *Alice's Adventures in Wonderland*
> —Lewis Carroll

It was an amazing realization to learn how many seemingly successful, high-potential leaders and even executives subconsciously hold themselves back, for reasons they may have carried with them for years, many since childhood. Unless someone intervenes to help them remove their self-inflicted roadblocks, neither they nor their companies are ever destined to attain their *Personal Magnificence*, as Garry Ridge would call it.

I'll share one story which floored many of my clients when we heard it from one of their leadership development peers, the president of a renowned and highly respected nonprofit. This president was a tall, slender, impressive-looking woman. Her stature naturally commanded attention whenever she walked into a room. She was unaware of the advantage this command presence gave her.

One day during one of our executive peer mentoring sessions, this executive confided she had always felt somewhat awkward when entering a room full of people or when standing in front of an audience. She deliberately tried to shrink herself by slouching a bit so she wouldn't appear to tower over the other women and some of the men. She said she had done this for years because she "just wanted to fit in."

Everyone else in the peer mentoring session was incredulous. They politely asked her what had caused her to feel this way. The president blushed and said she had been doing this since the fourth grade when, suddenly, she grew taller than all the boys in her class. She remained taller than most everyone else for the rest of her life, thinking she was a misfit. Because of this, she tried desperately to appear shorter so that she could better fit in with cultural expectations.

Interestingly, the tables turned, and she was stunned when virtually all the other female executives in the mentoring session told her, "Don't you realize most of us wish we were tall and slender like YOU? Be proud of who you are! Some of the most successful executives in the world are taller than everyone else."

This was a complete revelation to her. At that very instant, she sat up straighter, pulled her shoulders back and smiled, as though she had just become proud of herself. Her life changed as a result of that realization.

What a shame it took all those years for her to figure it out, but at least she finally did. Imagine, as successful as she had been to that point, just how much *more* successful she could have been (and her organization could have also been) all those years if she had cherished her unique stature or had at least been more comfortable in her skin.

Now, in the spirit of transparency, I will fill you in on my own little deep dark secret, one which took me years to admit to anyone.

I am an only child, and I grew up in an alcoholic home. My mother began drinking heavily shortly after my father bought a business in Bakersfield and moved the family there from Orange County. Although we seemed to be an average middle-class family before the move, my mother detested living in California's central valley. It was then she took to drinking all day, for days at a time. After that, our home was not a fun place for a child to be.

Once I completed sixth grade and until I entered high school, my father would take me to work with him during school holidays and summer vacations, primarily to get me out of the house. I earned one dollar a day filing customer paperwork and doing timecard accounting for the hourly work crews. I took pride in developing my grown-up work skills, and I was relieved to not be at home.

Eventually, my father rented an old beach house back in Orange County in hopes of bringing Mother out of her drinking binges. Mother and I then spent the summers and long weekends during the school year at the beach house while Father worked in Bakersfield. It became my job to look after my mother, not an easy task for a young teenager. From time to time,

I was so deeply embarrassed about my home situation.

Mother would enter a recovery home, sometimes for several weeks at a time. Meanwhile, I lived alone at the beach house. My father visited infrequently.

Out of sheer frustration one day, I drove myself to the local high school near the beach house and enrolled myself in school there.

The day I registered for school, I met another girl, Jenny, who was also enrolling that same day. Jenny told me her father worked for IBM. Jenny and I became fast friends. Each day after school, I spent as much time as I could at her house so I wouldn't have to go home.

I remember Jenny's dad saying to her mom one evening when he came home from work and found me, once again, sitting at the dinner table with their other four kids, "When did we acquire another daughter?"

My father had pretty much disappeared from the scene by the time my mother died at the end of my senior year. Thankfully, God sent me a lifeline. Jenny's family took me in as one of their own.

I was so deeply embarrassed about my home situation. I never told anyone about it. It took years before I even considered telling Jenny and my adoptive family what I had been dealing with all that time. They never pried. They just took me in, no questions asked, and gave me a place to belong and be loved. I was truly blessed.

Later, as an adult, I asked them, "How can I ever repay you for all you have done for me?"

They told me to pay it forward to others … and that's precisely what I have been trying to do ever since.

The point is this: You don't have to have grown up in a family like TV's *Ozzie and Harriet* or *Leave It to Beaver,* where the mom stayed home, happily making cookies. You don't have to have had a role model upbringing or obtain a PhD. Learn from your experiences and give life your personal best every single day. Do what you can do with what you have right now. Just do it.

No excuses. You may be amazed at what you can achieve with the talent and wherewithal you already possess.

Take a listen to the personal story of Southwest Airlines' Colleen Barrett:

I think I learned most of my basic values from my mom. We were a very poor family, and she was not well educated or skilled or trained. However, she had a huge, loving, caring heart and she raised three kids alone, even though she was married.

You learn from good leaders and from bad.

I think you learn from good leaders and from bad. My dad was not a role model of any kind, except for how I didn't want to turn out. She raised, fed, and clothed three kids by herself working as a keypunch operator. She'd come home with ink all over her fingers. She had a high school education.

She taught me The Golden Rule. I don't know if she ever used that expression, but she taught me that if you treat others with respect, you will get it back.

She also taught me not to be ashamed we were poor and didn't have a lot. If you were clean, you held your head high, and you worked hard, that's what life was about. You worked hard, and you appreciated what you got as a result of hard work.

She taught me a lot without ever acting like she was teaching me anything. What she taught me I didn't even realize she was trying to teach me. I finally understood many lessons later, in my early twenties.

She had such a huge heart. She loved people. As a teenage girl, because of my dad, I never wanted to bring people into our house. She would welcome anyone at our door. She often said, "There is always an extra seat at the table."

People would come by. I only realized many years later, sometimes that meant she wouldn't eat. She would just put a plate down if somebody came to the door when we were eating. We didn't have very much food. We were not paupers, but we didn't have a lot—what a lesson for a young person to learn.

She also taught me not to envy. I don't think I would have done that anyway; it's not who I am.

The other thing she taught me—which I didn't understand for the longest time—was you never know what goes on behind closed doors. I didn't understand that until I was a young adult. Then I got it big time.

She always told me, "Don't judge others. You don't know what they have been through or what has caused them to be this way." That taught me not to be afraid of people who looked different or acted differently.

I started as a secretary. No one wants that title anymore. But the truth of the matter is, it was the best learning platform. It was like anything else; it was what you made of it, and I loved it. I was lucky I had people who were willing to let me try anything I wanted to try. I was very blessed in that way; many people aren't.

I was raised through grassroots efforts. Now, some people pooh-pooh me when I say this today, but to me, that is what Southwest is. It's a grassroots effort.

Paul Spiegelman of the Small Giants Community shared this when Dr. Mark asked him, "Do you think your success is due more to being lucky than being highly degreed or highly trained?"

I think much of it has been luck and circumstance; I don't believe it has to do with training. I never read a business book until seven or eight years ago. I didn't go to leadership school.

I had experiences in my life which taught me how to build relationships with people and I think I used that, in a business sense, to build a successful business and then to learn over time what was important to me, what's important to my family, what's important to the people I work with. I'm just extending that.

Todd Wilcox of Patriot Defense Group, raised by his single mother, shared this story about his upbringing:

We were dirt-poor. We lived in what was called South of Gandy (SOG) in Tampa. Gandy Boulevard was the dividing line between the haves and the have-nots. My mother qualified for food stamps and aid for dependent children, those kinds of things, but she was adamant she would not do that. She put us to work as kids.

> **Take charge. Provide for yourself. Be accountable for the decisions you make.**

I started working when I was thirteen years old as a dishwasher, and I've been working my entire life ever since. It was self-determination.

My mother taught us accountability, to take care of ourselves, not be dependent on the people around you or the government, or dependent on the environment you are in. Lead the path. Take charge. Provide for yourself. Be accountable for the decisions you make. Those were things she taught us along the way and with a stern hand. As a single mom raising six kids, she was very hands-on, and she got the results she wanted.

Sometimes you take the good with the bad. You see in some people things you think will work, and you try them out later. Again, I've been fortunate along my last thirty-something years of being an adult. I've had these examples where I can test these things along the way. I've been in these leadership positions which have just allowed me to continuously refine my skills, my abilities, and my leadership style.

When I asked Todd, "Do you feel you are a different kind of leader because you've taken characteristics from so many others who somehow influenced you?" he replied this way:

> Yeah ... maybe ... that and the things I've read and educational experiences I've had along the way. I don't have a Master of Business Administration. I do attend Harvard Business School every year for an executive education program through the Young Presidents Organization, YPO. That's been helpful. Between the experiences I've had and the things I've learned, institutional knowledge-wise, I think I have a unique leadership style.
>
> I think what's unique about me is my pragmatism. I can go from being a micromanager, being very comfortable doing that with those who respond to that kind of management style, to being very hands-off with a lot of freedom, autonomy, and just basically saying, "Here is what we want to accomplish. Tell me how you're going to do it. Now go do it."
>
> I think what's unique about my style is that I can be pragmatic and move back and forth through the spectrum of leadership skills and methods as needed, based on whomever I'm dealing with.
>
> However, I've never been the smartest guy in the room. I never pretend to be. I think that helps when people give you a strong argument as to why you should do something you think might not be the right way. It's a little easier to accept if you're not so egocentric and egotistical.

As a child growing up in East Germany before and during World War II, Rein Preik of Chemcraft International had this to say about his early life experiences:

> As far as my upbringing was concerned, it had a lot to do with the pressures of the circumstances which we were under, under the Allied bombing, for instance, and the evacuations and resettlement from one country to the next.

I shouldn't say we were forced more into the family unit, but that's about the only thing I had. The only stability I had was family and faith. Within the family, of course, our parents were the ones bringing us up in the Christian faith. So, as you get older, you look back on it, and it becomes part of you.

When I asked him at what point after the war, he decided to leave Germany to make a living for himself, Rein responded with this:

It's one thing to make a living. What some people consider making a living, if you lived in Russia through the war and right after the war, making a living means you don't freeze to death. You have enough food to sustain you for today. So, when you consider making a living, I think you can make a living in many places. It doesn't matter how depressed the situation becomes. You still can make a living. In my case, I had a choice.

I had a conflict between what they taught in school and my belief system. I had to decide. To get ahead in life, you would have to accept the belief system that they were teaching you. I'm talking about the times after the fall of Hitler's Germany, after 1945.

Living in East Germany, the entire doctrine of Communism was taught to us. They were trying to present it to us in a very logical manner: the development of mankind, in different stages, and then ending up with Karl Marx' theory (Engels and Marx). We would try to fit into that square, into that form. That's what they were teaching us.

You had to show your commitment to them on an ongoing basis. They had special meetings. They had further education because they wanted to develop the young people so they could be used by the State. They wanted to bring the young people educated in that line of thinking into the government, into journalism, and other important positions.

Like in my case, when you are in a situation where there is a conflict (talking about making a living), you don't want to stay poor necessarily, if you have a choice. So, when, on one hand, you see freedom and opportunity, and on the other hand, you see a commitment to a system—you've got to decide. With my parents' blessing, I decided to immigrate to Canada, although I was barely 18 years old.

I immigrated to Canada on a little emigrant ship that had been a submarine tender ship. The British took over the ship. We were together with several hundred DPs (Displaced Persons). They could have been from Poland or Germany or wherever. I was with a cousin of mine. We were on this ship for probably seven or eight days in rough weather because the stormy season started in late summer.

We landed in Quebec City. To my surprise, I found out people there did not speak English. I had an English dictionary, but it didn't do me any good because they were speaking French. It just shows you how prepared I was to get to Canada. I didn't realize Canada was a real bilingual country where people there didn't speak English. I couldn't speak any English either, but I had a dictionary. So, I was fumbling around.

We took a train to Edmonton. We were in that train car for probably three or four days. It was a long way, and the train was very slow. Other trains had priority because we were all immigrants on this train, coming off the ship. The train would stop and unload two families in this city, then five families in the next city, and some people somewhere else. I ended up in Edmonton, Alberta, and tried to make a living. I tried to find my way there.

First, they put you in an overseas room for a week. We committed ourselves to work on a farm to help bring in the harvest. The farmer I worked for also had cattle and wild horses, but the objective was to help him bring in the potato harvest, which lasted six weeks, maybe. Then, we had twenty dollars in our pockets and were let loose. Then you try to make your way again.

When you are young, you experiment around. You want to see what it's all about by doing different jobs. I had several jobs related to what I had studied before, from the medical field to working in the mines, and so on. Eventually, you want to settle down because you come to a point in life where you must take on some responsibilities. You have to have a steady income from a regular job.

You try to go back to your education base and say, "Okay. What did I learn after ten years of schooling?"

Because those were war years, there were many interruptions. I had a two-year course in a technical school, where I learned to become a formulator in the paint business.

It always comes down to performance. First, I worked in the lab. I realized the people in the lab got a certain pay, but the people in sales got commissions. Their earning potential was more dependent on themselves, on their performance. I thought that was neat, so I appealed to the owners of the company, "I would like to go out and have my own territory and do my own stuff."

I successfully increased sales. After a certain length of time in sales, the technical manager quit. So, there was an opening there, and I decided I would like to come in and take over that position since I knew the product and had knowledge of the customers. I accepted that position.

When I started with the company, coming from Germany, I hadn't had much education. I had different jobs in different areas. I had to learn and find out what makes people happy, what were they expecting, and what my employer expected.

When Dr. Mark interviewed Howard Behar of Starbucks Coffee, he asked Howard to comment on his (Dr. Mark's) theory: "*To many transactional people, life is a deal—it's all about this deal and the next deal.*" Howard had this to say:

With this idea, "Everything is a transaction," we allow ourselves to take the humanness out of our lives, out of the things we do. We see things in the context of numbers, of rewards, of recognition, or whatever it happens to be. Every time we do that it's like taking a spoon—or in some cases a shovel—and digging out from our foundation of life ... of who we are as human beings.

Many times, we don't recognize it because it is like a little spoon. Every time we do it, we're taking out a tablespoon of the sand that holds us up. We lose track of what matters in life. I think we continue to see more and more of that, like "Let's get the deal done." This idea of digging out of our human foundation in life, one scoop, one teaspoon at a time, it slowly destroys us as human beings.

We make excuses for ourselves.

We make excuses for ourselves. We see things in the context of these transactions. Transactions are not always about money, although we see a lot of that. We look at it that way, in the context of money. Sometimes the transactions are about doing performance reviews. That's a transaction in a sense. It's rote. There is no humanity to it. There is no caring about it. It's just something we are supposed to do.

I have this idea. Rather than seeing people as customers or seeing people in their roles as bankers or teachers or authors or whatever, we need to see all people in the context of their humanness, of being a human being. Then, when you're dealing with somebody and whatever the job happens to be, whether you are trying to get a loan for your house or you are a banker trying to make a loan, you look at everybody through human eyes, through soft eyes. It doesn't mean you're not going to turn the person down. I'm not talking about that. But it does mean you come at it with a caring attitude, with a belief in him or her as a human being and a belief in yourself as a human being. That piece of it only requires practice.

We all get caught up in the transaction. We're all in a hurry to get things done. Being in a hurry adds to it. Slow down. Take your time. Think about what you are doing. Don't let yourself go there.

I was having a conversation with someone over the issue of technology and what technology allows us to do. We send emails. We're not talking with each other, even over a phone. It's very transactional.

I'm always laughing about my wife and me. We can be sitting right next to each other, working on our computers, sending emails to each other. It's transactions! We don't even take a moment to look into each other's eyes and say something. You can imagine what goes on in the work environment. It's even more of that.

What happened with the banking meltdown? The reason it melted down was the whole thing was a giant transaction. Nobody saw a human face in it at all. It was just loans being combined with other loans. No human beings buying homes. It wasn't someone thinking, "This is somebody's home. This is a house. This is where a family lives. We have a greater responsibility here."

So, the government steps in, and we create all these rules and regulations we shouldn't have to have. If you are thinking about people in the human sense, then it's not just a transaction.

Companies in our world today, particularly in public companies, we love this line on the P&L Statement. From quarter to quarter to quarter, it just goes up. Straight up. But no human being lives a life like that. Life is lived like this: It's herky-jerky. It's up; it's down. It's around; it's about.

We're always trying to mellow it out. We love this word: happiness. There's no such thing as happiness. I mean, there is happiness, but it's fleeting. It comes in little bits and pieces. What there can be is fulfillment. What fulfillment is about is disappointment, pain, anguish, happiness, joy, love, all those things. To have a fulfilling life, you have to experience all those things.

A business is exactly like that. It's representative of the human journey, this drive toward economic success. It's important, and I love it. I'm a capitalist pig. I love making money. I love turning in the numbers. But I never thought I had to do it on the backs of people. I never thought I had to blame others for lack of production or lack of making a number, whatever it is.

The board member I always looked to was the one who said, "Howard, you own this. There's nobody else who owns this, so get over it."

When I asked Donald Stamets of Auberge Resorts, "When, where, and from whom did you learn the values most important to you?" he responded:

I would say that's my mother.

It started at a very young age. We grew up with literally nothing. She was a single mother raising two boys. My father was still in the picture, but we were like weekend children, being passed back and forth. My mother taught me at a very young age about respect, integrity, and commitment to your word.

She was very ill at the time. When I was a young boy, I didn't know that. She was manic-depressive and became very sick after my brother was born. He was older than I am. I was a mistake. I wasn't supposed to be there.

It's only 20% what happens to you. It's 80% how you respond to it.

Growing up, the neighborhood kids thought I had the best life ever. Everyone wanted to be at our house because my mother was very manic, but we didn't know it at the time. We just thought she was the best mother in the neighborhood, and everyone wanted to be here. She's the one who did Halloween parties for everyone. She's the one who taught everyone how to dance. She's the one who taught everyone how to play tennis, how to live your life to the fullest every day, be positive, and show respect to others.

I was in high school when she started to become sicker. My biggest regret today is that I never had an adult relationship with my mother. When she was in high school, she was nominated "Best All Around," captain of the hockey team, captain of the tennis team, captain of everything. I try to live my life to be like her and make sure I am as positive as possible.

We have choices, as leaders and as people, when something happens to you. I always have said, "It's only 20% what happens to you. It's 80% how you respond to it." We have a choice. I think losing my mother (she went into a nursing home at the age of forty-four and had a stroke and died at the age of sixty-two) made me realize life is so precious and important I don't take anything for granted.

I'm just as positive as I possibly can be, using an individualized approach with anyone I meet because it's clear you're not going to meet everyone who has the same characteristics or values you have. But you still must go on, and you have a choice to make. I try to be positive at every turn, but it's my mother who gave me everything I have today.

I then asked Donald, "How has remaining true to those values and paying them forward contributed to your success in your career and your overall life?"

Donald said this:

I think it is 100% due to those values instilled in me as a child. I believe in business, or in any relationship you have, you must remain positive. You must have an open line of communication.

When I commented to Donald, "It sounds like you were trying many things and gradually stepped into leadership positions," he responded:

> Yes, at a young age. But wasn't I a leader at home? My brother and I, right?
>
> If you think about it—and again, I never really said it out loud until today—but with my father not in the picture, and my brother and I with my mother, we had to have a life. So, we had to lead. We had to direct where we were going. I had to get to school on time because my mother on some days was very capable of getting up and making us breakfast and getting us on the bus. Other days, she was not. Of course, at that age, you don't know what you don't know. I thought that was normal. I had to become self-directed at a very young age.

When I spoke to Teresa Laraba of Southwest Airlines and asked her the big question, "When, where, and from whom did you learn the values which have gotten you where you are today?" she summed it up like this:

> That's an easy one: from my mother. I had an interesting upbringing. My father was not a very kind person. My mother was an incredibly strong and caring woman. I don't even know if I realized how much until later in life.
>
> As we were growing up, I lost a sister early on. She passed away, and we had to bury her on my eleventh birthday. At the time, I think I was even more surprised my mother remembered it was my birthday and bought me a birthday present. It was a jewelry box. I still remember this.
>
> So, fast forward until I had my children and realized what gifts she gave me and my brothers. In the time where she was facing her worst loss, she was more focused on us than she was on herself. She was more focused on getting her kids through this than grieving for the loss of her child.

We were too young to put that together. It was a lesson I learned by watching her experience that. It has been the foundation of what has made me the type of person who thinks about everyone else before I think about myself. I believe that was a gift.

The key takeaway is this: No matter where you came from, no matter your upbringing, no matter your education, you have what it takes to create a WOW factor workplace.

It's solely up to you.

Soundbite FROM DR. MARK

What is your role as a parent? Probably most of all, it is to teach your child good judgment and the ability to make good decisions, especially when they are under pressure and away from you.

If developing good judgment is the outcome you're seeking, what is the best way to interact with your children so it will result in that? Just as importantly, what are the ways you interact with them and act around them (monkey see, monkey do) that prevent them from developing it?

If you do things for your children that they should learn to do for themselves, you will not only prevent them from developing judgment, you will prevent them from developing self-reliance, resourcefulness, courage, and commitment.

If you do things for your children that they should learn to do for themselves, you will not only prevent them from developing judgment, you will prevent them from developing self-reliance, resourcefulness, courage, and commitment. And when their peers from India, China, Russia, and Brazil—who have developed all these qualities—become their bosses, you will prevent your children from being promotable or possibly even hirable.

> If you tell them what to do, you will not cripple them as much as if you do it for them, but they will become dependent on you and not develop self-reliance.
>
> If, however, you believe in them more than your anxious need to be in control, if you ask them what they think they should do and why and if finally, you tell them to give it a try and report back, that will teach them self-reliance, independence, and judgment.

ACTION STEPS

1 Think about whether there might be some issue from your childhood you have been carrying around with you all these years. Has it been hindering you, or has it made you a better person or both?

2 Could you be a better leader if you accepted that issue as a leadership lesson and maybe even wear it as a badge of honor?

3 Now think about the culture of your workplace. Overall, would you define it as win-lose, lose-lose, or win-win? What are the factors that have made your workplace that way?

4 Is there something you have learned during your life that has contributed to YOU making it that way?

5 Is there something you might do differently to turn your workplace into a WOW factor workplace?

6 Consider what your workplace might be like if you were to drop the baggage you've been carrying around and give your own personal best every day.

EIGHT

It Takes Courage

If we can collectively invest and be courageous,
amazing things happen.
—BRITT BERRETT
former President,
Texas Health Presbyterian Hospital-Dallas

There is no reason why you, too, can't have a WOW factor workplace if you do what you can with what you have in order to create the conditions you have read about in this book. Your background doesn't matter. Your education level doesn't matter. You don't need to wait for those above you to "get it."

You can make it happen right where you are, for your piece of the action and those around you. You'll be surprised how far and fast the WOW factor can spread if you ignite it somewhere and gently fan the flames.

I was having tea one afternoon with one of my more astute mentees. As we talked, she took copious notes, seemingly of my every word, as she usually does (her act of notetaking helps her process what she hears). Then she abruptly stopped writing.

She looked at me and asked, "So, my big question to you is, what do you think I should do with my career now?" That was a big question, indeed.

I answered this way: "It all depends on your real priorities and what's most important to you. You must do some soul-searching and come to terms with those items for yourself. Then you'll be able to decide what you should do."

She seemed a bit perplexed, so I went on to explain, "You need to be honest with yourself about what is most important, in order of priority. Is it your career? Is it having a certain title? Is it the nature of the workplace around you? Is it your relationship with your life partner? Is it prestige or power in the workplace or the community? Is it making a difference for those around you?"

I encouraged her to write these things down and then try to put them in order of importance. I also warned her we each have a finite number of hours in each day. We cannot do everything. Sometimes you have to weigh your priorities day by day. Priorities can shift over time, sometimes in an instant, due to situations we cannot anticipate or control.

I then told her some of the key questions I make a habit of asking myself regularly, usually in the wee hours of the morning when the rest of my world is quiet and still.

- If I found out today that I only had a month left on this earth, what, if anything, might I regret?

- Is there anything I might regret having NOT done all these years, something I wanted to do but for whatever reason I allowed other priorities to get in the way?

- Is there something I did that I might regret because I failed to make amends properly?

- Is there someone I need to thank or apologize to, or someone to whom I can pay something forward?

- Can I change my behavior to improve the kind of responses or reactions I get from those around me?

- What do I have to do so by this time tomorrow, or next week, or next month, or next year, I could leave this earth with no regrets?

That is where you start.

The great thing is that it's never too late to make changes in your behavior to start making a difference.

Keep in mind—there is no failure in life. You or someone else might have unrealistic expectations, but you never fail as long as you learn from those experiences where you don't get the outcome you wanted.

My mentee deliberated on this for a moment and jotted down a few more notes. She then asked me, "What was the best decision you ever made?"

Wow. That was another big question.

> Start where you are. Use what you have. Do what you can.
> —Arthur Ashe
> First black-American tennis player selected to the US Davis Cup team

It was my turn to deliberate for a moment. I responded, "I don't know if there was any single best decision, but I can say the best decisions I have made throughout my life were the hardest ones to make. I say this because they were the decisions which changed my life, the direction I was heading in. These were the times I had to ponder all the things I just laid out to you: What were my life's priorities and what was most important? How would I live without regrets? Sometimes you cannot live entirely without regret for actions taken in the past, but you can take actions starting now to head in a new direction to make things a whole lot better for you and those around you.

"It was those times—when I honestly assessed my life's priorities and weighed what was most important to me—when I have made the best decisions, albeit some of them were quite difficult. These were the decisions which ultimately led to the kind of WOW experiences I have been most grateful for."

Here's a story about a high potential finance executive who had been hired away from a Big Four accounting firm by one of her multinational clients to serve in a vice president level capacity. However, for some reason, she did not live up to the expectations of her new division president in terms of leadership command presence. The division president placed her in our executive peer mentoring program for senior-level leaders, hoping to pull her out of her shell.

The first day she attended our executive program, she was reticent, yet she seemed to listen intently to every word and took copious notes. When it came time for her to speak to the group, she said little and quickly passed the floor to the next executive at the conference table. At the end of the meeting, she left hastily without saying much of anything to the other attendees.

She did not attend the next scheduled session. Instead, she called me at the last minute and explained an emergency had come up at the office which needed her attention.

After the session concluded, I called her division president and reminded him how important it was for her to attend if we were to have a chance of helping her step-up her leadership game. He seemed surprised she had failed to participate and indicated he knew of no emergency at her office. He committed to letting her know that our peer mentoring program sessions should be her #1 priority.

When she failed to show up for the beginning of the next session, I stepped out of the meeting after five minutes or so and called her on her cell phone. At least she answered the phone, but she uttered some excuse about being too busy to get away from the office to attend the meeting.

I replied, "Not attending is not an option. We are holding up our meeting waiting for you. Your tardiness is impacting everyone else here. Your office is twenty minutes away. Get in your car now and be here as soon as you can. No excuses."

Thirty minutes later, she arrived. For the next few hours, she was, once again, very quiet. She listened intently as each of the executives took turns sharing their current significant challenges. In turn, each executive asked clarifying questions of the one sharing the challenge. They each provided feedback and offered suggestions to the challenged executive, based on their own respective experiences.

When it came time for her to share her biggest challenge with the group, you could have cut the air with a knife. For a moment or two, she said nothing, thinking deeply about how best to express herself.

Finally, she said this: "I have to be honest with you. When I came here the first time, I was completely intimidated. I didn't feel as though I deserved to be at the table with such talented, knowledgeable, articulate, well-put-together executives. I felt ashamed that I could probably never measure up. I felt I didn't belong here, and I honestly didn't want to come back. Now I am here today, I hear each of you being so open and honest about your challenges and your struggles, the kind of challenges and struggles I can easily relate to. I have come to understand you are just like me. Now I realize if you are just like me, I can be just like you."

> **I have come to realize you are just like me. Now I realize, if you are just like me, I can be just like you.**

Wow. It took a big person to say that.

From that minute forward, the entire group welcomed her participation, and she embraced the program. Within a short time, she became a much more outgoing contributor. Her division president noticed a significant difference in her leadership abilities and her team's performance. The last time I checked, it sounded as though her organization was on its way to becoming a WOW factor workplace. She was on a new journey, inspiring those around her to come along.

> **Aspiration is not a destination. It's a journey we are constantly on.**

Dr. Mark asked Paul Spiegelman of the Small Giants Community: "Is there a difference between ambition and aspiration?"

Paul answered:

> I think "ambition" is something which defines us, as in being ambitious people. "Aspiration" might be a little more visionary,

in terms of something I aspire to become. I think aspiration is not a destination. It's a journey we are constantly taking. No matter where we are in our life, we always want something more. There is not a sign on the wall that says: *You have arrived.*

I recently sold my company after thirty years. I took no break to immediately think, "What's next?"

If I've had an impact on the lives of the people who work in my company, how can I now impact the lives of a bigger audience? How can I take the platform and the message I've been able to deliver and touch more people? I think that's aspirational. I'm only one person. I don't expect to change the world, but I'm going to do my part while I'm here to try to change as many people as I can.

When I speak, I talk about the events that happened in my business life, which took the business in a completely different direction than I had planned.

By no means do I feel like I've just succeeded because I had a plan, I had a goal, I hit the goal or exceeded the goal. It's all been very different than I ever anticipated. I never knew I would write books, or I would be a best-selling author, or I would have grown the company to the size it became.

I had examples of successes in my life: two uncles. Two of my uncles had businesses. One had a food manufacturing company, a small one in downtown Los Angeles. The other one had a company which took hotel linens and cleaned them, such as sheets and things like that.

Both had these family-owned businesses. At some point they sold them. I have no idea how much they sold them for, but it seemed to me they were enjoying their lives. They had grown these small businesses, sold them at some point, and were now enjoying the rest of their life.

That's all I ever aspired to: to be successful enough to grow a business and then enjoy my life. I only sold it because I know my kids are young enough it's unlikely I'll be around long enough to pass it along to them. It's not that type of business. It needed to be part of a bigger organization.

That's all I think about today. I put myself in the position to be like my uncles.

Now I may be doing a lot more, which has just come to me: the ability to teach others the things I have learned. I've been so incredibly fortunate to have been given the opportunities I've had.

I think a combination of it is "right place, right time" and listening, listening to mentors, listening to others...and being open to change.

I was not surprised to learn, sometime after we conducted the interviews for this book, Paul Spiegelman and Britt Berrett, former President of Texas Health Presbyterian Hospital-Dallas, were good friends. Britt summarized his leadership experience like this:

I know when I lead an organization, I care so much about the people. Not just about them as individuals, but the team they work on, the organization where we live, and the community in which we function.

Getting back to my life experiences in Peru, I saw how health care was delivered. I felt it was an indication of how they invested in their community. I hope as a leader I bless lives and unlock potential and when they go home, they're a better father, they're a better mother, they're a better brother, they're a better sister. That's the community in which I want to live.

There's a higher calling and purpose behind it all. I think great leaders are willing to invest because there is a higher calling and purpose in life. If we can collectively invest and be courageous, amazing things happen.

I asked Britt, "Does it take courage?"

It does take courage. It takes confidence. It calls upon a greater meaning in life. I think you can do your job and get through the day-to-day without caring. I think you can. I think it's hollow. At the end of your career, you look around and say, "Well, what did I accomplish? Who cares?"

Great leadership takes courage; it requires you to know who you are.

Covey talks about that in quite an eloquent manner, about leaving a legacy. I think the legacy is not, "Did you make the P&L?" The legacy is, "Did you build relationships that further a greater meaning and purpose for you, individually and collectively?"

That's why health care is so important to me. We get to take care of people and touch their lives every day. That's a divine calling in life. Colleagues outside of health care, I think they, too, can find that purpose and that meaning.

That's why Southwest Airlines is doing what they're doing. I think they consider it a great calling in life. I've heard them speak to that, on opening the airways, on opening travel for families and friends to connect. I think that's meaningful. But it does take courage, it really does. It's exhausting, too. It's not for the faint of heart.

It's not for those who are "kind of," "sort of," "sometimes," or "maybe." It's for purposefully driven people.

It takes an act of courage to define what you're good at, what you're not good at, what's important to you in life and what's not important to you in life.

I think you've got to ask yourself, "Where do I come from? Why am I here? What are we doing? Where do we hope to be in the future?"

Yes, you ask some very personal questions. Then you ask yourself, "Am I willing to pay the price? When I look out on the horizon, do I imagine where this organization will be?

Am I willing to pay the price to get there? Do I feel such a sense of angst, knowing what it would be like if we didn't get there?"

I feel that way in my organization. I'll wake up in the middle of the night, thinking, "What if my loved one came here? What would the experience be? Does it give me such angst knowing one of the departments is not working as it should?"

Yes, there is a message: I think it takes courage.

I think great leadership takes courage. I think it requires you to know who you are. It takes an act of courage to define what you're good at, what you're not good at, what's important to you in life and what's not important to you in life. When you have the courage to ask yourself those questions, that unleashes potential. It also requires you to have the courage to care about people and open yourself up, and do so in a very purposeful way, to bless their lives.

I had the opportunity to ask the late Teresa Laraba of Southwest Airlines, "What is one thing you wish you knew when you took this position?" She told me this:

I don't know if it would have changed my mind, but it is interesting you ask that. I love this company so much. I love to work with the people I work with day in and day out. I did not aspire to do a lot of external speaking and to really be standing out, speaking on behalf of Southwest in a much larger, more global atmosphere.

I have enjoyed it, and I'm learning to embrace it, but if someone had told me I would be doing this interview with you, for example, or speaking at conferences, or just the amount of external exposure, it would have taken me back a little bit. I never thought I could Google myself and find so much information, which is somewhat frightening the first time.

I have enjoyed it. But it has also put so much more emphasis on the fact I must honor what Southwest Airlines has become. I have to make sure when I'm out there speaking about Southwest, that's what I am portraying. It was very humbling to realize I was going to stand in front of groups or speak with people. I was going to share information with thousands of people, and they were going to look at me and say, "Is she leading Southwest Airlines?" and "Is that what Southwest Airlines has in a leader?"

I'm proud to say it is. However, it was a little frightening in the beginning to realize how global and how out-front the role was going to be, especially for somebody who didn't want to seek that in the first place.

I followed up by asking Teresa, "If someone had told you that up front, would you have done the same thing?"

She replied:

Yeah, I would have done the same thing. I'm probably better off that I didn't know, and it just snuck up on me.

I might have sought a little more self-education on some of the public speaking and some of the public presentations. I have been very fortunate, again because I work with great people who have helped coach me and have given me feedback along the way.

I asked Donald Stamets, now at Auberge Resorts, to reflect on an earlier time when he reported to a toxic manager. Donald shared this when I asked him, "What do you do when you wake up one day and realize 'I don't want this anymore'? Does it take courage to make a change?":

My bonus was eighty-five percent of my salary. I made a lot of money in those three years. It's not about the money. If it were, I'd still be there, but I would be miserable and cranky. That affects your personal life and that's not good. Life is too short.

I learned from my mother that you've got to make tough decisions. There's life beyond what you're currently living. You've just got to find what's going to make you feel comfortable and happy ... because life is too short not to enjoy happiness.

Most of the examples of WOW factor workplaces we've looked at in this book have been in industries most people are familiar with, places we as consumers might interact with in our day-to-day lives. But let's not forget there can be WOW factor workplaces in organizations like the military, too.

Colonel Debra M. Lewis (US Army, Retired) had a remarkable 34-year military career, which began with her attending the Military Academy at West Point, in the first class to include women. A Bronze Star Medal recipient, Colonel Deb ultimately led three brigade/battalion-level commands, including the oversight of 850 employees responsible for constructing, operating, and regulating military and civil works projects in the Seattle District. Earlier, she led 500 employees in military and civil works projects in the Philadelphia District.

One of her last commands was in charge of the Baghdad and Al Anbar Provinces for the US Army Corps of Engineers, leading the $3 billion reconstruction of central Iraq. Following the concept of courage, I asked Colonel Deb to share a bit about that experience.

Despite IEDs, mortar attacks, and snipers everywhere, we traveled with our security detail. It was an exciting time to be an engineer and part of the reconstruction effort. Basic infrastructure had been sorely neglected under Saddam Hussein. My years of blazing new ground at West Point and throughout my career shaped me to be mentally tough *and* caring, able to deal with extreme adversity, high pressure, and constantly changing conditions.

Never alone, I did it with a team of people I considered a dream team. I focused on listening to their needs and helping them be successful. It was incredibly rewarding to know you could influence your people in positive ways and make a huge difference in the lives of others because of better infrastructure.

When I asked Colonel Deb what made the units reporting to her such WOW factor organizations, she reflected:

I want to share a secret I learned. Everything that is a serious or important subject doesn't have to be handled in a dignified manner. The opposite is true. If you want to encourage needed change, a smile can lighten a burden and move mountains. Smiles also don't cost a penny. What if it were true that we have all the resources we need to resolve our toughest issues? What else would it require? Everyone working together!

Over my life, I learned to embrace the bad times, even when I felt beaten down. I'd wonder what lesson I was missing; otherwise, it might

Rather than making some big splash, if we lead our lives each day from the heart, where every choice we make has this in mind, we will be far more successful.

happen again (and sometimes did). Bad things which happen to you can also reconnect you to what you care about most and help you appreciate the people in your life.

When you care deeply about others, about what's going on around you and in our country, the military becomes a very honored place which embodies service above self. While staying positive in the real world takes skill, life is easier when you serve a higher purpose.

No one serves in uniform their whole life. When you get older, you must retire. I decided that once I left the military, I would look for opportunities to help even more people. The military is only one type of service.

When we think about our WOW factor workplace leaders, heartfelt leaders, it's not about a single role or job you do. There's so much potential throughout our lives, whether it's at home, at work, the first career we start with, or other ways we contribute to society. Everybody can have a positive impact, but it takes leadership, courage, skill, and self-discipline.

The more we understand and are in touch with our hearts, especially what we care deeply and passionately about, the easier it is to successfully navigate the steady stream of negative forces which exist in our world.

It takes courage to lead with your heart. It takes courage to be in the line of fire, where people are going at each other and then may start attacking you. But by doing it with caring and love, you can make an enduring difference. My criterion was this: if I can change just one life, then I will have made a big difference.

Rather than making some big splash, if we lead our lives each day from the heart, where every choice we make has this in mind, we will be far more successful. It's not just with those we most care about and love but includes every connection and every new friend we make along the way.

Soundbite FROM DR. MARK

Question: **What do you think is the most valuable insight to have?**

Answer: **The insight into what you say and do because it effects your results, your reputation, and your relationships.**

In treating people over the years, an exercise which has proven helpful has been asking them to imagine their personality as a circle. In it are the parts of them where they are trying to prove, show, hide something, or please someone else.

I then ask them to now imagine erasing all those parts and then tell me what's left over, because what's left is *them*. All the other parts have to do with reacting to others versus expressing who they truly are.

A surprising number of these people smile at me and reply, "Not very much."

The result of this exercise: If you can eliminate the *prove, show, hide, please* parts of your personality, you may discover a calling which has been beckoning to you for years.

ACTION STEPS

1 Ask yourself, what is stopping you from creating WOW factor conditions in the workplace where you are today?

2 Do you know the impact you make on those around you? Ask them to find out. Be sure to ask them to be honest with you ... and then, listen.

3   Once you have done this, write down your answer to this question (be honest with yourself): What is most important to *you,* in order of priority:

- Your career
- Your title
- The nature of the workplace around you
- Your relationship with your life partner
- Prestige or power in the workplace
- Prestige or power in your community or beyond
- Making a difference for those around you
- Something else?

4   Now you know how to ignite the flames, so what can you do to create WOW factor conditions within your organization? How about in your life?

5   Now, write down the first three steps you will take to create WOW factor conditions right where you are, starting today.

NINE

The Time for WOW Is Now

Creating a "Best Place to Work" begins with you.

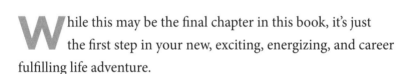

While this may be the final chapter in this book, it's just the first step in your new, exciting, energizing, and career fulfilling life adventure.

Let's quickly review what you have learned about creating a **Best Place to Work.** It's a WOW factor workplace:

1. with a best-ever boss.

2. that takes your breath away … in a most satisfying way.

3. where you and those around you love what you do.

4. where you and your teammates take great pleasure and pride in envisioning WOW together.

5. where high expectations are clearly defined, mutually agreed upon and achieved, time and again, day after day.

Armed with this knowledge, you now have what it takes to make that most important *next* step. Whether you choose it to be just a baby step or a flying leap, creating a WOW factor workplace begins with *you*. Don't wait for your boss to change … *you* make the change.

Take charge. Start where you are. Use what you have. Do what you can. You own this.

Imagine. WOW *is* within your reach. Tomorrow might just be the day when you'll jump out of bed, for the first time in a long time (or maybe ever), with an I-can't-wait-to-go-to-work attitude … like you've just won the lottery.

Rest assured, Dr. Mark and I will be here, cheering you on. We can even facilitate a workshop for your team or conduct a conference for your company or professional association if that's what you need.

No matter what, keep learning. Ask questions. Listen. Read. Keep up the dialogue. Check out our website, *HeartfeltLeadership.com*. There are blogs, shared stories, and additional resources that can help you take your leadership skills and your team's performance to the next level, to a **Best Place to Work** level. And be sure to read the sequel to this book, *Heartfelt Leadership: How to Capture the Top Spot and Keep on Soaring*.

Now … go out and WOW the world.

Index

About the Author

Deb Boelkes founded Business World Rising over a decade ago, with a dedication to accelerate the advancement of high-potential businesswomen, and men, to the top of industry-leading, "Best Place to Work" organizations.

During her 30 years of experience building and leading Sales, Marketing and Professional Services organizations within global Fortune 150 technology firms, Deb earned her long-held reputation as a high energy, heartfelt leader who gets things done.

Having ascended her own career ladder within male-dominated corporations, Deb knows only too well the challenges women, in particular, can face in their efforts to achieve career and corporate success. She knows how certain attitudes and behaviors can undermine personal advancement, team performance and inter-departmental cohesion. She also knows the real culprit … and solution … emanates from the heart of leadership.

Deb is as passionate about the messages conveyed in this book as she is about helping organizations and rising stars establish and achieve their own visions of success. In addition to her vibrant focus on public speaking; producing Best Place to Work and Heartfelt

Leadership symposiums; and mentoring high-potential heartfelt leaders; Deb continues to enjoy interviewing and learning from other heartfelt leaders across the country and around the world.

She has worked with clients as diverse as Experian, Merrill Lynch, Smashbox Cosmetics, Segerstrom Center for the Arts, Toshiba, and Junior Achievement.

Deb received her bachelor's degree in Business Administration and her MBA in Management Information Systems from the University of Rhode Island. She lives on Amelia Island in northeast Florida with her husband, Chris. Together, they have three grown sons and three granddaughters.

About Mark Goulston, M.D.

Dr. Mark Goulston, co-founder of Heartfelt Leadership, is a business psychiatrist and the author of seven prior books … with his book, *Just Listen: Discover the Secret to Getting Through to Absolutely Anyone,* now the top book on listening in the world. As a result, Dr. Mark has become one of world's preeminent experts on empathic listening.

Also the founder of *@wmystglobal,* Dr. Mark is an executive coach, mentor and confidante to leaders from start-ups to the Fortune 100. He speaks globally on leadership, communication and influence. He hosts the critically acclaimed podcast, *My Wakeup Call,* where he interviews influencers about their personal journeys and wakeup calls that led them to where they are now. He is regularly quoted and featured in print, radio, podcast, television including: *Harvard Business Review, Wall Street Journal, Fortune, Forbes, Inc, Fast Company, Business Insider,* CNN, BBC-TV, ABC/NBC/CBS News, and he was the focus of a PBS television special on listening.

How to Work with Deb

Deb Boelkes' greatest value lies in inspiring leaders to embody a new kind of leadership style … one that fosters an inviting and energizing culture and espirit de corps; one that produces and sustains greater employee and customer loyalty; one that consistently delivers a healthy impact on the bottom line … heartfelt leadership.

Neither heartfelt leadership nor the creation of an engaging Best Place to Work culture can be learned through standard training techniques. Passions must be stirred and inspired. Hearts must be reached. That's what Deb does best.

Deb gives enlightening keynote speeches. She produces eye-opening symposiums, conducts energizing workshops, and consults with executives and high-potential leaders at all levels.

Deb Boelkes and Dr. Mark Goulston, together, orchestrate riveting Heartfelt Leadership symposiums for corporations, universities, government entities, not-for-profit organizations, and professional societies. Consider sponsoring a Best Place to Work or Heartfelt Leadership symposium as a new way to attract and retain the superstar leaders of tomorrow.

There has never been a better time to take your leadership and your organization to a whole new level … to a Best Place to Work level … through heartfelt leadership. Contact Deb today.

Deb Boelkes

FOUNDER, BUSINESS WORLD RISING, LLC

Deb.Boelkes@BWRising.com
Office: +1 (904) 310-9602

DebBoelkes.com | BusinessWorldRising.com
HeartfeltLeadership.com

LinkedIn.com/in/debboelkes/

Twitter: @DebBoelkes

Look for the next books in the series

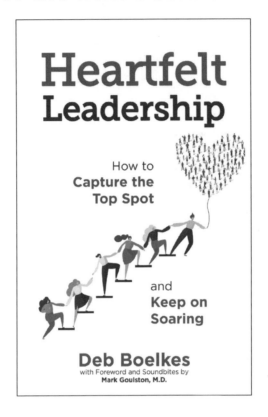